THE OBEDIENT CHILD

The Obedient Child

*A Practical Guide for Training
Young Children in Confidence,
Character, and Love of God*

Ken Wilson

SERVANT BOOKS
Ann Arbor, Michigan

Published by Servant Books
P.O. Box 8617
Ann Arbor, Michigan 48107

Cover design by Michael Andaloro
Cover illustration by Whitney L. Lane / Image Bank

92   10 9 8 7 6

Printed in the United States of America
ISBN 0-89283-613-X

Library of Congress Cataloging-in-Publication Data

Wilson, Ken, 1952—
    The obedient child.

    1. Child rearing—Religious aspects—
Christianity. 2. Children—Religious life. I. Title.
HQ769.3.W56   1988   649'.1   88-18275
ISBN 0-89283-613-X

Table of Contents

Foreword

I'VE KNOWN KEN AND NANCY WILSON for many years now, and I continue to be impressed with how they are rearing their children.

The practical and pastoral teaching on training young children that Ken writes about in his new book, *The Obedient Child*, is something that he and his family have lived out and continue to live out in their daily life. It is producing very good fruit in the lives of the four Wilson children.

In fact, the teaching in this book is being lived out by hundreds of families in the ecumenical Christian community that both the Wilsons and my family are a part of, The Word of God in Ann Arbor, Michigan. And it is producing very good fruit, helping parents form confident, obedient, respectful, and godly children.

Building on what I wrote in *Husbands, Wives, Parents, Children*, Ken explores in depth the training of young children, a topic that is not treated with the same detail in my book. Ken doesn't avoid the difficult issues or give unrealistic, untried advice. I can enthusiastically recommend his new book to everyone seeking greater wisdom in the all-important task of rearing young children.

At a time in our culture when the disintegration of the family seems to be accelerating, such a book is welcome indeed.

Ralph Martin
Author of *Husbands, Wives, Parents, Children*

Introduction

"YOU CAN'T DO THAT. I'm the boss!"

My wife Nancy was pushing her grocery cart through the canned goods section and turned around to see who was making the declaration.

She saw a little girl who looked about three years old, sitting in a grocery cart as young children do, addressing her mother who was walking away from the cart. Again, the declaration: "You can't do that. I'm the boss!"

The mother turned, walked back to the child, looked her straight in the eyes, and with an endearing pinch on the cheeks replied, "That's right, honey, you're the boss."

Something's been happening to parents. We're forgetting how to be in charge. We feel ambivalent about exercising authority and confused about how to do it. We are losing our instincts for training children. We know that we should love them, we know that we shouldn't neglect or abuse them, we are concerned about their sense of security. But we're losing our instincts for training them—for modeling, leading, teaching, and insisting that our children do certain things—that they adopt certain attitudes and develop certain values. We're especially tentative about training them to be obedient and respectful toward us.

Over the past several years I've had very close contact with a large number of parents who are raising children. These men and women are disciples of Jesus: they are themselves committed Christians, and they want to raise their children to be sons and daughters of God. Many are mature believers with a

commitment to the biblical teaching about raising children—
teaching that stresses the importance of obedience, the need
for loving discipline, the responsibility of parents to train their
children. But in spite of this, they find that putting it into
practice doesn't come naturally to them. They don't have a
"feel" for it.

Even many who were raised in stable homes haven't had
much experience being trained. They have fathers who are
excellent mechanics, mothers who are great homemakers, but
they didn't learn much about these things from mom and dad.
Life was too busy, the kids were always absorbed with their
friends, and the TV was an ever-present distraction. They can
remember their parents being displeased or angry or upset
with them, but they can't remember being disciplined by their
parents in a firm, reasonably consistent, and effective way. Also
those parents I know who come from families which suffered
some serious dysfunction—an alcoholic parent, serious mari-
tal discord, sexual or physical abuse, serious emotional dis-
orders—certainly don't have a wealth of positive experience to
"give them a feel" for raising and training their own children.

This book is meant to be a help to parents and other
influential adults who are disciples of Jesus and who want to
raise children as much as possible according to the biblical
teaching. It is a book designed to help parents of young
children. The examples and practical advice given have in mind
children up to the age of six or seven. And it is meant to help
parents train their children, especially to train their children to
be obedient and respectful. Who knows? Maybe the lady in the
grocery store with the three-year-old boss for a daughter (or
daughter for a boss) will read this book and take another look
at the way she's resolved the power struggle.

Rather than lay out the fundamentals of Christian family
life, I will assume the reader is familiar with these and agrees
with them. Ralph Martin's book, *Husbands, Wives, Parents,
Children,* (Ann Arbor, Michigan, Servant Books, Revised

Edition, 1983) covers these fundamental principles well. Many of these principles have historically been accepted among Christians and are widely accepted today. Others have been accepted for centuries among Christians, but have fallen out of favor in recent times.

For example, I will assume that the reader understands and accepts the biblical teaching about the role of the husband as head of the family, his responsibility to provide loving leadership, to exercise his authority under Christ, and the role of the wife to submit to her husband's direction. I will assume the reader is convinced that children ought to obey their parents and that spanking is one legitimate form of discipline (among others) when used wisely and in love. Most people these days have lots of questions about how these principles are put into practice, and hopefully some of these questions will be addressed in the book. But if you are opposed to these principles, I should warn you that you might find the book a little irritating.

I am a father and a pastor, not a psychologist, so I will be writing from a pastoral perspective. The covenant community that my family belongs to has about 1,500 children. In one recent year, 100 children were born to community members. I've had the privilege of living in close proximity to many of these parents and children, and I have served many of them as a pastoral leader. Three of these kids live next door to the right of us, three live next door to the left, and four show up for dinner every night at our house: my son Jesse, 18 years; and my daughters Maja, Amy, and Judy, ages 16, 10, 8 respectively.

With an eye to helping parents put the material in this book into practice, I've organized it so that married couples, single parents, and groups can apply the teaching a chapter at a time. At the end of each chapter, I have included two sections. One is titled "Putting It into Practice," and the other is titled "For Group Discussion and Support." The first section is designed to help readers apply the material in the chapter to their own family life. Wherever possible, I've tried to identify a few concrete steps that will help married couples and single parents put the material into practice.

As you work through the material and make changes in your approach to child rearing, I advise you to seek the counsel of your pastor or pastoral leader. Of course, the amount of input you seek will depend somewhat on your circumstances and your relationship with those in pastoral authority in your local church or Christian community. But the key principle here is that pastoral care, as expressed in the local body of Christ, can be a significant source of protection and guidance for your family. For example, consulting with your pastor may help you identify problem areas or solutions you would otherwise overlook. It may also prove helpful in confirming or raising questions about a course of action you're considering in a specific area.

Finally, remember to pray for your spouse and your children as you apply the material in this book. Make it a daily practice. Remember to seek God's will for your family when you make important decisions about raising your children.

But a word of caution is in order. Making changes in child rearing is a challenging task. Individual family circumstances will vary widely. Not all of the exercises suggested will be helpful or even manageable for every situation. So please use the "Putting It into Practice" sections flexibly. Select the exercises that promise to be most helpful and are within your reach. Let the others pass. Also take enough time to implement changes when you use these exercises. I recommend that you tackle only one area at a time as well.

The second section, titled "For Group Discussion and Support," is designed for groups who want to support their members as they read and study the material presented in the book. Prepare for your discussion by reading the chapter and, if you like, jotting down any notes. The questions for group discussion are only meant to serve as discussion starters. Again, use this section flexibly, depending on the needs of your group. If you spend a full discussion session on one question, that's fine. Depending on the nature of the group, you may also want to use some of the material from "Putting It into Practice" to spark discussion.

I recommend that you connect up with your local church or Christian community if you do decide to go through the material with a group. In fact, you may want to organize your group under the auspices of your church or community, if that's possible. Support and encouragement from the local body of Christ will be invaluable in implementing these teachings on child rearing.

Also you'll want to develop a format, an approach to leadership, and a set time for group meetings. In my sections titled "For Group Discussion and Support," I suggest that you close each group discussion with a time of prayer. You may also want to begin your meetings with a short time of prayer. After the formal close of your group meetings, you may want to consider having a period of informal fellowship with refreshments as well. This will give group members an opportunity to get to know each other better in a relaxed atmosphere.

For those who wish to use these two sections for application, I recommend you begin with the last chapter. Most readers will probably want to jump right into the chapters dealing with child-rearing issues like obedience and respect. But if you are able to make a more significant investment in working through the material, there is a decided advantage to beginning with the last chapter. This chapter recommends that each husband and wife begin to meet regularly as a team to discuss child-rearing issues and then make decisions. Getting that practice in place will go a long way toward helping you apply the rest of the material.

Indulge me, please, in a word of appreciation to those who have contributed in a special way to this book. First of all, I wish to thank my wife Nancy. She has been a great source of wisdom and support and has, I believe, a special knack for raising young children. Nancy has been a crucial co-worker in developing this book. I originally presented this material to a few families whose commitment to raising their children for Christ has been a great encouragement to me—the Rykowskis, Hausraths, Flemings, Sauters, Hiles, and Jens. Peter Williamson, Steve Clark, and Ralph Martin have all been sources of much personal encouragement, good advice, and inspiration in Christ. A number of pastoral leaders, both men and women, and other members of the covenant community to which I belong, The Word of God, have inspired and encouraged me in more ways than I can begin to count. And of course, I am thankful to my parents, Glen and Blanche Wilson, and my four children who by the grace of God are daily reminders to me of the blessing that God intends children to be.

I would welcome any comments from readers, especially those who have used the "Putting It into Practice" and "For Group Discussion and Support" sections. Simply write me in care of Servant Books: P.O. Box 8617, Ann Arbor, Michigan 48107.

ONE

What the Bible Says about Training Children

I N MY FIRST YEARS AS A FATHER, there were certain words associated with the parental role that I didn't like. When I heard these words I became suspicious, ill at ease, concerned. You know the words I'm referring to: discipline, obedience, spanking, punishment, training. My thinking about these words boiled down to this: if you did a decent job loving your kids, you wouldn't have to worry about any of these things.

But something began to happen that inspired me to take another look at these concepts. I wish I could say that my primary motivation came from encountering these ideas in the biblical teaching on child rearing. That gave me some motivation, but not enough to get down to serious business. What really moved me was the fact that my little boy was turning into a brat, contradicting all my self-generated opinions about child rearing!

He was three years old, and he was frequently unwilling to do what he was told—reasonable things, mind you, like "Stay in your bedroom please," or "No, we can't buy any toys even though we are passing through the toy department." I was impressed by how miserable life could become in a home! I can still remember my surprise when I realized I didn't have the slightest idea how to keep him in the bedroom, if he didn't happen to be in a state of deep slumber.

I thought kids really had to go off the deep end to make life miserable, but it seemed like much of his behavior was considered normal by most people. You know what I mean: you are in line at the checkout counter, and a toddler begins to whine and squirm and cry because mom didn't respond to the high-impulse item display near the cash register—displays that seem to make more money from manipulative toddlers than from reasonable consumers. The poor mother is embarrassed, and you're embarrassed for her. The lady behind her says reassuringly, "Look's like it's getting close to nap time!"

"No," says the mortified mom, the honest type, "it's two hours before nap time."

Almost as if it's your civic duty, you take a shot at helping her out, "He's probably just hungry."

"No," she says, her voice flat with desperation, "we just had a snack at the snack bar."

"Sometimes sugar will do that to a child," the helpful cashier chimes in, but it doesn't help either.

Nobody had told me how miserable life could become when a normal, healthy young child doesn't get his every wish granted. And it seemed that my son was also a participant in the misery; he wasn't having fun becoming a brat.

So in spite of all my resistance to words like discipline, obedience, spanking, punishment, and training, I was ripe to reexamine my child-rearing theories when a friend gave me *Dare to Discipline* by Dr. James Dobson.

Looking back, I can identify three sources of my discomfort. I think many of us are affected by these three concerns. My first concern was rooted in my feeling (and it was a feeling more than a reasoned response) that a child-rearing approach which embraced the biblical teaching that includes discipline, training, and punishment would produce frustrated, oppressed, rebellious children who couldn't experience a loving relationship with their parents.

Second, I am ashamed to admit that I was afraid of what

other people would think if I adopted an approach to raising my kids that was not traveling along the mainstream of modern thought. It is one thing to acknowledge that Christians need to follow Jesus who is himself the way of true wisdom, even if that means being different. But it is another thing to be different in very specific and noticeable ways. The biblical teaching urges parents to use physical punishment as part of a training process. That didn't tickle my university-trained ears, nor did it tickle the ears of people who were very important to me.

Third, I was "double minded" about what my responsibility as a father really was. I say double minded because, in fact, I held two contradictory opinions at the same time. On one level, I thought that I was responsible as the Scripture says to raise my children in the "discipline and instruction of the Lord." That is, I was called to raise them to be Christians and to live the Christian way of life. But at the same time, I was deeply influenced by the notion that a parent should only provide a loving and stable relationship so that when a child "came of age" he could choose what he wanted to be—if he chose to be a Christian, fine; if not, that was fine too. But he shouldn't be overly influenced or "programmed" one way or the other. I could hope that he would choose to be a Christian, but it wasn't fair to "stack the deck."

My parents never pushed me toward a particular career or set of interests, and I appreciated that. Somehow I felt that the same "hands-off" approach was a noble one to take in the very personal matter of what a person believes and how he lives as a result of that belief. When I put these two opinions together, I came up with a hybrid that isn't uncommon among Christians: the best way to train my children in the discipline and instruction of the Lord is to take a hands-off approach, leaving them as free as possible to go the way they were inclined to go.

The Command to Train

In order for Christian parents to follow the way of Jesus in our role as parents, we have to make our peace with the words that Jesus respected as the words of God. And God's Word is very clear in commanding us to train our children.

> Train a child in the way he should go, / and when he is old he will not turn from it. (Prv 22:6)
> Fathers, do not exasperate your children; instead, bring them up in the training and instruction of the Lord. (Eph 6:4)

We are to lead our children through a process of training aimed at shaping a particular way of life. Another word for training is the word "formation." Formation is an especially helpful word because it brings out the idea of giving a form or shape to something. In other words, training (or formation) doesn't simply pass along information in a random fashion, but it is always concerned to produce something with a particular form. For disciples of Jesus, this means we are to train our children "in the discipline and instruction of the Lord." We are to train our child in the "way he should go"; a whole way of life is in view here, not just beliefs or values but beliefs lived out in concrete actions, characteristic responses, and patterns of living.

This background can help us understand what Paul meant when he said, "Fathers, don't exasperate your children, but bring them up in the training and instruction of the Lord." What is Paul getting at? Often we think that when he says "don't exasperate your children," he simply means "don't be too demanding." Certainly Paul is saying that parents shouldn't abuse their authority. Being overly demanding is a problem parents should avoid. But it's worth noting that Paul doesn't say, "Don't exasperate your kids; instead, be easier on them." He says, "Don't exasperate them; instead, bring them up in the training and instruction of the Lord." This suggests another concern. Namely, we are not to be purposeless in our child rearing or misguided in what we are training our children to be and do.

Do you know how frustrating it can be when someone is exercising authority over you—giving you directions and correcting you—without a clear purpose in mind? The direction given seems to be dictated by personal whim. The person's correction seems motivated by particular things that happen to irritate him or her. That's not training—it's simply the capricious exercise of influence. Just as frustrating is being trained for a purpose you were simply not made for. Like the father who pressures his son (a son who is not strong in analytical aptitude) to become a lawyer. Fathers, don't exasperate your children, but bring them up with a particular purpose in mind, the purpose for which they were created, "the training and instruction of the Lord." This "discipline" or "teaching" of the Lord is the only way that leads to life. It is the only way of escape from unending misery.

The Training Context

In the New Testament, training is a process which involves a personal relationship between the trainer and the person being trained. The most obvious training relationship in the New Testament is the relationship between Jesus and his disciples. The disciples weren't just students attending classes taught by Jesus. They were in a personal relationship with their master. They lived with him, they traveled with him, they helped him, they ate with him, they spent a great deal of time together. And there was a great deal of love between them—Jesus for his disciples and the disciples for their master. While Jesus brought them into friendship, it wasn't a "buddy-buddy" friendship. Jesus was in a position of authority over them, and the disciples were not overly familiar with him (notice that the disciples always used a term of respect when addressing Jesus: master, teacher, Lord, not "Hey, Jesus").

Paul's training of a younger man, Timothy, is another New Testament example of a training relationship. Again, we see a close personal relationship characterized by deep affection.

Paul writes to Timothy, "Recalling your tears, I long to see you, so that I may be filled with joy" (2 Tm 1:4). And within this relationship, we see Paul exercising authority over Timothy. The letters of Paul to Timothy are filled with Paul's direction, admonishment, correction, encouragement, and advice to Timothy.

The relationship between father and son (parents and children) is understood as a training relationship of deep love which includes the exercise of authority, including painful punishment.

> In your struggle against sin, you have not yet resisted to the point of shedding your blood. And you have forgotten that word of encouragement that addresses you as sons: "My son, do not make light of the Lord's discipline, / and do not lose heart when he rebukes you, / because the Lord disciplines those he loves, / and he punishes everyone he accepts as a son." Endure hardship as discipline; God is treating you as sons. For what son is not disciplined by his father? If you are not disciplined (and everyone undergoes discipline) then you are illegitimate children and not true sons. Moreover, we have all had human fathers who disciplined us and we respected them for it. How much more should we submit to the Father of our spirits and live! Our fathers disciplined us for a little while as they thought best; but God disciplines us for our good, that we may share in his holiness. No discipline seems pleasant at the time, but painful. Later on, however, it produces a harvest of righteousness and peace for those who have been trained by it. (Heb 12:4-11)

The elements of training highlighted in this passage are correction, rebuke, and punishment—the painful elements of training. They are by nature unpleasant, but they lead to peace in the future.

Again, notice how this training, including the painful aspects of training, is presented in the context of a committed personal relationship. In fact, this discipline is a **mark** of the father-son relationship. Without it, there is no relationship. Note also that the training is viewed as normal—every child should expect it and receive it as a sign of favor. It is motivated by loving concern for the child's well being.

Now there is something important to understand about the biblical view of training (which includes discipline, correction, and punishment): it is an expression of grace! Listen to the apostle Paul addressing this very point:

> For the grace of God that brings salvation has appeared to all men. It teaches [trains] us to say "No" to ungodliness and worldly passions, and to live self-controlled, upright and godly lives in this present age, while we wait for the blessed hope. . . . (Ti 2:11-14)

The word translated "teaches" in the New International Version (NIV) is the Greek word, *paiduo*. *Paiduo* is the same word used in Hebrews 12:6 where it is translated "discipline." The grace of God—that unmerited favor that brings us salvation—also trains and disciplines us. Training that includes discipline, correction, and punishment is not opposed to grace. In fact, it can be an expression of grace, an extension of favor.

Physical Punishment

The Scripture unambiguously assigns a positive function to physical punishment in child rearing. Of all the books in the Bible, the Book of Proverbs has the most to say about childrearing. Proverbs emphasizes the responsibility of parents to train their children. Within that training process, the role of physical discipline is integral.

He who spares the rod hates his son, / but he who loves him
is careful to discipline him. (Prv 13:24)

Discipline your son, for in that there is hope; / do not be a
willing party to his death. (Prv 19:18)

Folly is bound up in the heart of a child, / but the rod of
discipline will drive it far from him. (Prv 22:15)

Do not withhold discipline from a child; / if you punish him
with the rod, he will not die. / Punish him with the rod /
and save his soul from death. (Prv 23:13-14)

The rod of correction imparts wisdom, / but a child left to
himself disgraces his mother. (Prv 29:15)

Discipline your son, and he will give you peace; / he will
bring delight to your soul. (Prv 29:17)

To say that the Bible assigns a positive role for physical
discipline in child rearing is probably stating it too mildly.
Indeed the Scripture views withholding physical discipline as a
sin against the child; it is a failure of love, something that
harms rather than helps him or her.

Physical Discipline and Child Abuse

It is not uncommon today to equate all physical discipline
with child abuse. Child abuse is a very serious problem in many
homes, one that no civilized person can take lightly. But there
are important differences between proper physical discipline
and child abuse.

Child abuse is usually an expression of frustration, anger, or
hostility. The abuser is often someone who was himself abused
and who finds himself caught in the same pattern. For some, it
may be a compulsive behavior similar to the compulsion of an
alcoholic for alcohol. It is not the thoughtful response of
someone who is engaged in a training process. Instead it is a
seriously disordered pattern of behavior, often accompanied
by powerful emotions out of control.

The physical abuse of a child brings physical (as well as

emotional) injury to the child. Proper physical punishment involves pain, but it shouldn't be injurious to the child. An effective spanking should provide a sharp sting which is over quickly—but it should not produce broken bones, bruising, or bleeding.

When should you be concerned that physical discipline is becoming abusive? When it is fueled primarily by anger, especially anger that is not under control; when you find yourself throwing a child down, vigorously shaking him in frustration or causing physical injury apart from the transient sting of a good spanking. Physical punishment is in danger of becoming abusive when it is primarily reactive (swatting a child without thinking about what you are doing or why) rather than deliberate and thoughtful. If you find these things happening, it is time to step back and seek help.

Embracing the Responsibility to Train

A friend of mine once told me something I've heard more than a few times from parents: "I just can't see myself as a disciplinarian." Most parents in our culture know exactly what that feels like. The word itself conjures up negative images for many: the stern assistant principal who handled all the "discipline cases," the marine drill sergeant who strikes fear in the hearts of the recruits. And yet God clearly charges us with the responsibility to train our children and that formation process isn't complete without discipline, including physical punishment. This is not something we can avoid without avoiding some of the most emphatic teaching in the Scripture on the parental role.

Do not conform any longer to the pattern of this world, but be transformed by the renewing of your mind. Then you will be able to test and approve what God's will is—his good, pleasing and perfect will. (Rom 12:2)

Isn't that just what we need in this area—the renewing of our minds so that we can approve what God's will is? We view the exercise of discipline as restrictive, oppressive—something that strangles and inhibits life. But in Christ, the exercise of parental discipline is a pathway of life for our children.

Let's humble ourselves under the teaching of Christ and consider his thoughts higher than our own. Let's lay aside our opinions and fears—formed as they are by a world in rebellion against God, unwilling to submit to his training—and open our minds to the transforming influence of God's Word.

In a very concrete sense, the growth of our children in obedience depends on our own obedient response to the Word of our Father.

Putting It into Practice: What the Bible Says about Training Children

> If you haven't read the Introduction, you missed some important pointers on how to use this section. Check it out before you tackle these exercises.

1. Sit down with your spouse and schedule a weekly time when you can discuss the material in each chapter.

If you are a single parent, schedule a time when you can give undistracted thought to each chapter. Keep notes as you read the material that is pertinent to you and your children. If you have a supportive friend who is able to work through the material with you, consider when you could get together to discuss the exercises in "Putting It into Practice."

Jot down the time and place for these weekly discussions:

2. The author mentioned three concerns that made him uncomfortable with the idea of training (pp. 16-17). Which of these concerns, if any, could you most identify with? Note it below:

_____

_____

3. Do you have any concerns about the use of physical discipline not mentioned in the chapter? What are they?

_____

_____

_____

4. Review the list of proverbs in the chapter that speak of physical punishment in childrearing (p.22). List three positive results of physical punishment mentioned in the proverbs.

_____

_____

_____

For Group Discussion and Support

1. Share the specifics of your plan to set aside a weekly time to discuss the material in each chapter with your spouse, or if a single parent, a weekly time to consider the material or discuss it with a friend.

2. Share one concern that you have about the biblical view of training, discipline, and punishment. Then share anything

helpful you found in the biblical teaching on child rearing that helped you put that concern into perspective.

3. Pray together as a group. Ask God to give you his mind about training and disciplining your children.

TWO

The Role of Favor and Affection

HAVE YOU EVER OBSERVED how senior physicians train medical students or residents? A group of doctors will go on medical rounds—visiting hospitalized patients, reviewing their charts, and discussing their treatment together. You can tell who the senior doctors are by the length of their white coats—the longer the coat, the more seniority. The long coats train the short coats by grilling their juniors with questions about the patient under consideration: "What can you tell me about this disease? How does the patient's kidney function complicate his treatment? What are the chief side effects of the medication he's receiving? What complications should we be looking for?" The instructor will ask questions until the student runs out of answers. Then the long coat keeps asking questions to demonstrate just how much the student has to learn, pointing out to him the potentially grave consequences of his ignorance.

Some students wilt under the treatment. It's too much for them; it devastates them. But others actually thrive. They rise to the challenge, motivated to learn more and more. For them it's painful but productive. Those who thrive are the ones who have somehow developed a basic sense of personal security and confidence.

I am by no means advocating the training of physicians as a model for training children. But have you ever noticed that children who respond well to the discipline of their parents, even discipline that others might call "strict" or "demanding," are often the children who are also developing a basic sense of security and confidence? They are not fearful or apprehensive, but at peace, confident, secure.

The relationship between security, confidence, and discipline is a two-way street. Children who have learned that there are limits placed on their behavior, limits enforced by consistent training which includes discipline, are often better equipped to succeed when faced with new challenges. They gain security and confidence from the growing awareness that they need not be subject to every internal whim. In this sense, effective discipline develops security and confidence in a child.

But effective discipline alone isn't enough. Paul writes in Colossians:

Children, obey your parents in everything, for this pleases the Lord. Fathers, do not embitter your children, or they will become discouraged. (Col 3:20-21)

Along with effective discipline, there are three keys to building up children so that they do not become discouraged or "lose heart." In this chapter we will focus on the first two: favor and affection. In the next chapter we will consider the third, building confidence.

Favor

When God brings us into the life of Christ, we begin to taste something that is indeed food for our spirits and water for the parched ground of our souls: the favor of God. This is the favor that Jesus knew, for example: "This is my Son ... with him I am well pleased" (Mt 3:17).

In Christ, we are no longer an offensive smell, but a pleasing aroma in heaven. As we enter into this favor, we are motivated as never before to hear him say, "Well done, good and faithful servant." This is a key to God's care for his sons and daughters—to give us a taste of his favor, to let us know that we are pleasing to him, even while we are still in the process of being sanctified, purified, and purged of much that offends him.

Because children are born uncivilized, because, as the proverb says, "Folly is bound up in the heart of a child," children normally need a great deal of correction. And correction involves at least some indication of displeasure. But with God as our example—and he is our example since we are to be "imitators of God" (Eph 5:1)—we can also express favor to our children. In fact, we should be looking for opportunities to express favor, to let the children know that we are pleased with them.

So we look for opportunities to enjoy our children. And we tell them when we enjoy them.

"I'm glad we had a chance to go to the store. That was a good time we had together."
"I enjoyed having you around to help me with that project. You were good company."

We look for opportunities to "catch them doing it right." And we let them know when we have caught them doing it right by saying, "Well done."

Isn't this how Paul did it—whom we are also called to imitate as he imitates Christ? Have you ever noticed how Paul starts so many of his letters with a word of favor, of commendation, a "well done"?

Even when he writes to the Corinthians, who were doing a few things to displease him, a few things requiring correction, discipline, and punishment, he begins by expressing his favor:

I always thank God for you [that is an expression of favor] because of his grace given you in Christ Jesus. For in him you have been enriched in every way—in all your speaking and in all your knowledge—because our testimony about Christ was confirmed in you. Therefore, you do not lack any spiritual gift as you eagerly wait for our Lord Jesus Christ to be revealed. (1 Cor 1:4-7)

We know that Paul was sorely vexed by the problems among the Corinthian believers, but he did not become so preoccupied with their faults that he forgot to recognize the good things. He took the time to say, "Well done."

Andrew Murray in his worthwhile book, *How to Raise Children for Christ,* makes the point that we should especially express our pleasure when the children have had to overcome disinclinations to do what is right. For example, your son is just learning to share his toys with others and a little friend asks for a turn with his truck. The owner of the truck pauses, furrows his brow in consideration of the request, and says to your surprise, "Sure!" When that happens, pull him aside and say, "I saw that! It wasn't easy for you to share your truck, but you did it anyway. Good for you!"

Instead of making as big a fuss over things such as good looks or natural athletic ability, we should express our favor concerning the things that are pleasing to God. We reinforce values by the things we honor. I happen to think my daughters are strikingly beautiful, but what would it say to my daughters if I highly praised them for their physical beauty, which is of little importance to God, while giving them only cursory praise for an act of kindness or faithfulness?

Some Things to Purge

Some correction requires an expression of disfavor to get the point across, but certain expressions of disfavor are not appropriate. They tear down, rather than build up a child.

1. Avoid unfair characterizations. When a child misbehaves, don't launch into a series of name calling: "Turkey!" "Jerk!" "Bad boy!"—statements which amount to sweeping generalizations about a child's character. Better to identify the offending behavior or attitude and then speak simply and directly about it: "You should never bite your brother—that's mean and I won't stand for it."

We should also be careful about the use of humor which is bent in a negative direction. Children are often incapable of sorting through the subtleties of indirect or negative humor. You may use a term like "you little nincumpoop" endearingly, but why play around with humor that is so easily misunderstood? Humor of this kind often contains a seed of hostility, however small or subtle, and this can be communicated underneath all the smiles and warmth.

2. Unresolved displeasure. "For his anger lasts only a moment, / but his favor lasts a lifetime" (Ps 30:5). This is a profound insight into the attitude of God toward the objects of his love: momentary anger, lasting favor. His favor doesn't interrupt his anger toward his sons and daughters; his anger interrupts his favor.

Have you ever experienced lingering or vague displeasure directed toward your child? That's like asking a marathon runner if he's ever gotten a blister on his foot.

We had a dog named "Lad" who was not the apple of my eye, but the pain of my behind. He once ate an avocado that was clearly out of reach on the counter. Have you ever met a dog that would eat an avocado? A whole avocado? This was an irritating animal. I could always tell that I was feeling a vague or lingering displeasure toward one of the children when I would lapse into calling the child "Lad" by mistake.

The times when we get into lingering displeasure directed toward our children may be clues that some objective attitude or behavior on the child's part needs to be dealt with. If so, take the hint supplied by the fact that you are calling your son or daughter by your dog's name and examine more specifically what's bothering you. Address that issue, rather than letting it linger unattended. You may decide to correct or forbear, but examine it and decide how to respond.

Lingering displeasure may be a symptom of a failure to bring correction or punishment to closure. As a good salesman clinches the deal, we should bring it to the point of decision and concrete action, rather than leaving it in the realm of vague intention. If this is happening, put your energy into dealing with the issue rather than letting it linger unattended.

Lingering displeasure directed toward a child may be your problem, not his or hers. You may be mad at your spouse, angry with the circumstances, tired and overworked, or your displeasure may be spilling over from some other source. Deal with the underlying source of the anger.

3. Yelling. There are some people who seem to think that you can waltz through a few decades of child rearing without ever raising your voice. I wish they were right, but sometimes a little extra volume is necessary. However, yelling at the children as a regular occurrence, a normal part of the script, is usually not helpful.

This is not a precise matter. There are some cultural variations in what is considered "yelling." I have a fair amount of British in the blood (my Victorian grandmother tried to purchase a ticket for the *Titanic* maiden voyage, but they were sold out). For my family, yelling and raising your voice were synonymous. My wife is part Polish, and in her family yelling and raising your voice were two very distinct ways of communicating. At any rate, yelling as a normal means of addressing a child's behavior isn't very effective. Often it simply helps foster an atmosphere of vague displeasure. In many settings, when mom or dad do a lot of yelling at the children, it is a sign that the kids are not being disciplined effectively. The yelling is replacing clear-cut, effective discipline. May the God who created us to be like him, help us to be like him. "For his anger lasts only a moment, / but his favor lasts a lifetime" (Ps 30:5).

Affection

Before a child understands the mysteries of God's love, his heart is prepared for this knowledge through the affection of parents and others who are close to him. The affection we show our children is not just part of our relationship with them, it is their first taste of the grace of God. While the grace and love of God cannot be reduced to affection, there is an affectionate and tender dimension to it.

"How I longed to gather you as a hen gathers her chicks under her wings," Jesus said as he looked over the city of Jerusalem. "Oh Israel, you are inscribed in the palm of my hand; how could I forget you?" This is God speaking through the prophet Isaiah, revealing his tender affection for his people.

God not only loves and favors his children, he expresses his love and favor—he speaks of his love and favor. We have the hope of being like him because we have had the divine nature planted within us. Let's express our affection for our children as God does—liberally and generously. Holding children, kissing them, smiling at them, expressing affection in any of a thousand ways can be important clues to them adding up to the understanding that God loves them.

It is also important to say "I love you" to the children, helping them to express the same to you. This isn't automatic; it comes easily for some, but not others. Like many other things, they need to learn how to receive and give this kind of verbal affection. It helps to start very early and continue as a child grows. My teenage son, who is no lover of "mush," will say, "I love you, Dad" in response to a similar expression on my part or on his own initiative. This sometimes happens at bedtime—a pattern that began when he was very young.

It is good to find ways to let children know that they are special in your eyes. Telling your child "You are the apple of my eye" can be one way of expressing that special place he or she has in your life. Special doesn't necessarily mean "exclusively special"—all your children can be special, each in a unique way.

Look 'em in the eye. There is a saying which goes: "The eye is the window to the soul." Jesus said, "If your eye is clear, your whole being is full of light." ("His eye is upon you...," a phrase from the psalms, is a sign of God's favor.) The eye seems to be a pathway for intimacy, for knowing and being known. Eye contact can implicitly communicate to a child that he is known—a comforting thought suggesting the possibility that he can be loved.

With our four children, I've been impressed how each child responds differently to various forms of affection. Like ballroom dancing, parents need to lead in a way that the children can respond. What works for one child won't necessarily work for another. Our third child, Amy, was especially responsive to affection by being affectionate in return. But Judy, our youngest, just didn't seem very interested in affection. It would have been easy to neglect Judy's need for affection, and Amy could easily have incorporated her younger sister's share. But we decided to pay attention to helping Judy give and receive affection. Over time, Judy has become increasingly affectionate herself and increasingly responsive to the affection of others.

A friend of ours noticed that her daughter was positively repelled by physical affection. She would shrink back in response to a hug and seemed to despise being kissed. The mother simply made a point of touching the child affectionately in a very unobtrusive way—a brief hand on the head or the shoulder. Over time her daughter began to "warm up" in her response to physical affection. Her mother didn't overwhelm her with anxious affection, but she gently led her daughter in responding to affection.

Another child might respond to a more straightforward exhortation to be more affectionate: "Don't be so stingy with your affection; give your dad a big hug back when he hugs you."

Beware of the tendency to decrease physical affection as

children get older. Our culture tends to view affection as something reserved for little children. We do need to modify expressions of affection as children get older, introducing a greater measure of dignity, but it is a mistake to let affection die out over time.

Children can become less responsive to affection as they spend time in environments where affection isn't practiced or valued. Parents should look out for this and not simply yield to pressures for less and less affection. One family insists on a certain minimum of affection between family members, including siblings (they have a pattern of hugging each other after dinner; everyone is expected to participate).

We often think of affection as the domain of the mother. Mothers do seem to have a special role to play in giving affection, but it is not an exclusive role. The father's affection is also important. A father's affection helps counter the natural competition that can develop between dad and his son. It can also keep a measure of tenderness to complement the father's role in discipline, as well as help the son learn how to develop brotherly relationships with other men. A father's affection is important in reinforcing a daughter's acceptance of her femininity. Too little affection from dad can be a factor in girls seeking affection from the wrong sources.

Putting It into Practice: The Role of Favor and Affection

1. Select one of the inappropriate expressions of displeasure—the one you winced over because you've heard yourself using it. Take the following approach to this one matter:

- First, admit that you don't have it all together as a parent and note this as just one example. Welcome to the club.

- Second, ask God to remove this fault from you.

- Third, share it with your spouse or a close friend. Be very specific about what the expression of displeasure is.

2. Make an inventory of two things you appreciate about each of your children. Note the specifics down in the space provided:

(Child 1) _____

(Child 2) _____

(Child 3) _____

(Child 4) _____

(If you have more than four kids find more space to complete your inventory!)

In the next 24 hours, (extensions are granted if you have more than a couple of kids) tell them what you wrote down. Or mention these things to someone else in the child's presence.

3. Plan to say "I love you," or words to that effect, to each of your children once each day for the next three days. If you need a reminder, write it down in your calendar or put a note on the refrigerator (in code, of course) and do it.

4. Try this out for the next birthday party in your home:

• Ask every member of the family to write out on a 3 x 5 card a few things they admire or appreciate about the person whose birthday is being celebrated.

• Mom or dad will need to help the little children fill out their cards. ("I like when he plays tag with me.")

• Collect the cards at the dinner table. Select someone to read them aloud to honor the birthday boy or girl (or mom or dad).

For Group Discussion and Support

1. Share your thoughts and decisions from "Putting It into Practice."

2. Share with the group one thing that you do consistently to express favor or affection to your children.

3. Identify someone you know who does a good job at showing affection and favor. Describe this person in action.

4. Discuss what you've learned or observed about distinguishing the sin from the sinner while correcting your child's behavior.

5. Turn to God in prayer. Ask him for the grace and strength you need to show favor and affection to your children in a consistent way.

THREE

Building Confidence

O NE OF THE CHARACTERISTICS OF A WELL-TRAINED CHILD is confidence. This is only natural. As an expression of grace, training really does provide encouragement, hope, and strength to a growing child. The child who is given direction and training (in contrast with the child who has been "left to himself," Proverbs 29:15) will be a child who is growing in confidence.

A good deal of this confidence comes as a child is trained in obedience, but it is also important to build confidence in other ways. This growing confidence, in turn, will help the child to receive training in obedience without becoming discouraged.

A Believer's Confidence

First of all, we must be clear about one thing: *the confidence of a believer is not rooted in self but in God*. There is a great deal of contemporary concern with building up one's confidence. But it is all built on the sand of self-reliance.

Paul expressed the believer's confidence when he said, "I can do everything through him who gives me strength" (Phil 4:13). Paul was a man who was deeply convinced about the unreliability of his own independent resources, of his autonomous self. "I know that nothing good lives in me, that is, in my sinful nature," he wrote, declaring the bankruptcy of self-reliance (Rom 7:18). Yet Paul had confidence in God. And this confidence in God was expressed by an expectation that Paul would succeed in what God called him to do because he knew that God was with him to strengthen him.

That's the kind of confidence we want to foster in our children: faith that God is there for them, to strengthen them—confidence that God will enable them to do what he calls them to do. The early experiences of meeting and mastering the mundane challenges of life provide a foundation for confidence—confidence that God is one who is near to help them do and learn what they need to do and learn.

The biblical model for learning is one that builds this kind of confidence. It is the model of discipleship: a master-student relationship, where the student lives near the master, has a personal relationship with him, observes him doing things, helps him do things, does things while the master observes and corrects and teaches and helps, and eventually is able to do what the master does. The student who learns in this way doesn't get built up in a confidence rooted in self and marked by pride; rather, the student develops a confidence characterized by humility and gratitude—confidence based on the knowledge that he or she has received something from someone else.

The disciples of Jesus don't become self-reliant as they learn to do what Jesus does because they know that what they are passing along is only what they have received. Their confidence, in other words, is rooted in God's grace. It is real confidence—characterized by boldness, by the expectation of success, by freedom from paralyzing self-doubt and fear. It is confidence in God: I can do all things through Christ who strengthens me.

The more we take the biblical approach to teaching and learning with our children, the more they will grow in this kind of confidence. And it is the tasks and learning opportunities of daily living that provide the fodder for this kind of teaching and learning. Much of it we do very naturally, without even thinking of it: helping the children learn to walk, learn to talk, learn to eat. We are in a relationship with them, they observe us doing these things, they begin to do these things. We encourage, teach, coach, help, correct; and before long they are walking and talking, and are able to eat in the presence of others without incurring outrageous dry cleaning bills.

There is a set of challenges that children face which are not necessities such as walking, talking, and eating at the table. They are more like "optional challenges." These are the things we can pay some attention to in order to help build the child's experiential base for confidence. For example:

Learning to ride a bike. Do you remember what it was like, at the age of six or seven, to learn how to ride a two-wheel bike? You were prepared for this miracle by an apprenticeship on your tricycle. Then you spent time on the intimidating two-wheeler with training wheels attached. But eventually, it was time to do what seemed to you impossible.

To the logic of a six-year-old, it does appear impossible, except for the fact that so many others can do it. How can balance on two thin wheels be maintained? Learning to ride a bicycle is an excellent opportunity to learn a lesson about the invisible realm, to trust what someone says who is trustworthy more than you trust your own feelings. Eventually, through trial and error, you learn to rely on something you can't see—the law of inertia: objects in motion tend to stay in motion. If you try to sit still on the bike, you fall over. But if you can get the thing moving, it's more difficult to fall.

When a child learns to ride a bike with coaching from mom or dad or an older brother or sister, or a friend of the family, he is in fact learning an important lesson in trust. It is a lesson which prepares him for the fact that God is near and available to help him do what he cannot imagine doing.

Learning to throw a ball overhand. At least in American culture, learning to throw a ball is a surprisingly useful skill. It is one of those key skills that help children engage in a whole set of sports and games. Over the years I've taken time with each of my children to teach them how to throw and catch well.

Doing simple chores. Even small children should have their own chores around the house—simple tasks they do regularly. A four-year-old girl, for example, may not be able to set the table for dinner, but she could be given the job of placing the ice cubes in the water glasses or passing out the napkins. Having regular, daily chores that children can learn and master helps to build their confidence.

Set 'Em Up to Succeed

A good trainer will set up his student for success. There are three keys to this. The first key is timing. A good teacher will choose to pass along a new skill when the child is ready to succeed. Jesus didn't send the disciples out in pairs to proclaim the gospel and demonstrate its power until they were ready for the new challenge. He gave them time first to learn the message of the kingdom themselves, to observe him in action, and to assist him in simple ways in the work. When it came time to send them out, he knew that it would stretch them, but he also knew that they were ready for the challenge.

If we press too much too soon, a child may actually master a given skill a bit earlier than he or she might have, but often at the price of confidence. Mastering the skill is accompanied by more tension, more frustration, more anxiety. For example, many parents are highly invested in getting their children toilet trained as soon as possible. Besides the obvious motivation, there are often powerful family pressures to teach the new skill. Relatives may begin to ask you whether or not your child is toilet trained as soon as he reaches whatever the magic number is in their mind (for many it is 18 months). Is he using the potty yet? No? Well what are you doing about it? Toilet training can become the first major challenge with social pressure attached!

You start receiving books like *Toilet Training in Seven Days: Do or Die* from concerned friends and relatives.

Mothers can become anxious about living up to someone else's expectations and before long toilet training is the pivotal issue between mother and child. How's little Robert doing today? Well, he's achieved 75 percent control in number one and 25 percent control in number two, up 5 percent in both categories since yesterday. That kind of pressure simply isn't worth it to achieve toilet training a few months earlier. If it takes a longer period but the child experiences the fact that with help he can succeed at the job, the extra diapers are a good investment.

The guiding principle here is that the wise parent will choose to pass along a new skill at a time when the child is most likely to succeed.

The second key to setting up children for success is breaking the new skill into a series of smaller, achievable steps. For example, if you want to teach your daughter to set the table, depending on her age and ability, break the job into smaller steps that she can accomplish with some ease. For a few days, have her set out the napkins until she's folding them neatly and placing them consistently in the right place. Then have her set out the napkins and put the glasses in place until she's mastered that. Then add the silverware and so on until she's learned to set the table well. Your encouragement and correction will be much easier for her to absorb, and she will gain a taste for the fact that with help, she can master new skills.

The third key to setting them up for success is modifying the learning environment to encourage success. It was easy to teach my first-born anything athletic. I had no one else to throw the frisbee with, so it was easy to be patient with him. When my daughter came along and began to participate in learning these new skills, I noticed that she became more easily frustrated by failure. I realized that without giving the matter much thought, I was trying to teach her how to throw and catch along with her older brother. By comparison, she was inept and it was tempting to be less patient, less encouraging of her small successes. It was a discouraging environment for her. Things improved considerably when I worked more individually with Maja until she developed basic competency in the skill she was learning.

Confidence is Catchy

Children also learn confidence by osmosis. That is, they absorb it from those around them. They learn confidence from our example. That's good news if you are the apostle Paul, fully convinced that you can do all things through him who strengthens you. But what if you have a long way to go in growing in confidence?

First of all, if you haven't already, it's time you faced up to the fact that your children don't have perfect parents. You didn't have perfect parents and neither do they. We are part of a messed-up race, bent out of shape, missing the mark. Our redemption and sanctification have begun, but the job isn't finished yet.

Remember? Our confidence in raising our children isn't rooted in ourselves, it's rooted in God. He's the one who has promised to demonstrate his faithfulness from one generation to the next. I want to be the best father I can possibly be, but I also have to remember that my children have a Father who can make up for the fact that their earthly father is imperfect. I don't offer this as an encouragement to passivity, but as a reminder of reality and an antidote to insanity!

Having reminded us of reality, there are some things we can do to build confidence in our children in spite of our own weaknesses in that area.

1. Don't forget to expose your child to the things you can do confidently. You may not have confidence speaking before groups of people, but if you can supervise the practical arrangements needed for a large group meeting, let the children see you in action and bring them into helping you. You may not have the confidence to sing in front of people or to instruct adults in singing, but you can still encourage your children to sing. I know some parents who cannot carry a tune in a bushel basket, but they sing. And their children can sing and usually better!

At any rate, give some thought to the things you can do with confidence. It usually takes some thought because you've probably learned to take it for granted. Remember to make it a point to expose your children to these skills with a view toward passing them along.

2. Let your children see you learning new things by relying on God for help. I'm not much of a handy man, and sooner or later my kids wise up to this fact. They notice that Mr. Rykowski does in ten minutes what it takes forty minutes for Dad to do. But over the years, I've gotten better. Mr. Rykowski and some other friends gave me a Readers' Digest "how to fix it yourself" book. At first I thought they were trying to tell me something about their availability to lend a hand.

But they weren't and the book has been a big help. More than a few times the kids have heard me praying for help on a project as I looked through the book and then eventually thanked God for getting me through something I had never tackled before. The lesson is that your kids can learn how to do something by watching you do it.

3. Arrange for children to learn from others. Usually we think of this only in terms of arranging piano lessons or swim lessons. But there are other important skills and work habits and character traits that our children can pick up from others. We've had a number of different single people live with our family for a year or two over the years. The children have been able to learn all sorts of things from the variety of people they've had closer contact with.

Guarding Your Tongue

Finally, if we are going to build up our children in confidence, it is important for us to be confident in God's nearness and help. We should be confident in his willingness to help us and our children to be what he wants us to be and to do what he wants us to do. Guard your heart and your tongue in this area.

Do you ever catch yourself complaining to someone else about a child's failures in front of that child? It's easy for parents to be pretty loose with their lips when it comes to speaking about their children's faults and failings, often in the guise of light-hearted speech: "Mary is forever losing things— that girl would lose her head if it weren't screwed on to her shoulders."

You may have your doubts about a child's ability to do what is called for, but don't tell him or her. Comments like, "I don't think he'll ever catch on" are overheard more than you might imagine and can become self-fulfilling prophecies. The problem with these complaints, of course, is that children who hear them believe them often enough. They may buy the lie and find themselves trapped by the deception which saps their own faith. Instead, we need to "speak the truth in love" about the challenges confronting our children: they can do all things through him who strengthens us.

Putting It into Practice: Building Confidence

1. Select a chore to teach your child. Make it something simple enough for a young child to learn, something like:

• emptying the wastebaskets for garbage day

• placing the napkins at each table setting for dinner time

Once you've identified a chore, break it down into smaller steps. (For example, get a large plastic garbage bag and empty the wastebasket into the garbage bag. Learn which rooms have wastebaskets to empty. Tie up the garbage bag after you are finished. Take it to the trash can outside.)

List the steps for the chore you've selected below:

(1)_____

(2)_____

(3)_____

(4)_____

(5)_____

Now decide when to begin the training process. Take a few days in a row. "Walk it through" with your child. Take him step by step until he has mastered the chore.

2. List three things that you would like to train your child to do in the next year.

(1)_____

(2)_____

(3)_____

For Group Discussion and Support

1. Share one thing you have trained your child to do. What was it? How did you do it?

2. Mention something specific that you occasionally do which works against training in confidence.

3. End the session with group prayer. Thank God for the small steps forward taken by each individual group member in child rearing thus far. Ask God for the confidence and faith only he can give you in raising your children. Close with prayer for one another's requests.

FOUR

Obedience and Respect

R EMEMBER THE THREE-YEAR-OLD I mentioned in the intro-
duction? The one in the grocery store who scolded her
mother with the assertion: "You can't do that. I'm the boss!" If
you had witnessed the exchange in the canned-goods aisle, no
doubt you would have wondered what the mother was doing
wrong to raise such a nervy kid.

You've probably wondered the same thing any number of
times—perhaps when observing your own children in action,
but certainly when encountering other people's kids! You're
driving down a residential street where some older school-age
children are playing a street game. As you pass, they step out of
the way, but just barely out of the way, and they throw a defiant
look at you. In the rear-view mirror you see one boy shaking his
fist at you and the other making a gesture with one of his
fingers. This isn't the first time you've observed something like
this and you wonder, "I sure can't remember this happening so
often twenty years ago, or didn't I notice? What's with these
kids?"

Or remember what happened last night in your own home?
You asked your daughter to pick up her toys before bedtime.
She said, "Do I have to?" You said, "Yes, you have to." She said,
"Dad! It'll take forever." You said, "No, it won't take forever. It
will just take a couple of minutes." The conversation continued

like this longer than you'd like to admit. Then the phone rang. Your last words to your daughter were, "I want you to pick up those toys now." Five minutes later you returned to the living room, and there is your daughter playing blissfully—the toy area still a mess. Without really thinking it through, you decide it's not worth the trouble; and you pick the toys up yourself after your daughter is tucked into bed.

Have you ever wondered why kids act like this? The answer to that question cannot be boiled down to one response. There are a lot of reasons kids act like this. Sometimes the home environment is filled with tension and anger. Everyone crabs at everyone else, and the kids are just playing by what they think are the rules: "This must be how we love one another." The child may suffer from some emotional dysfunction. He may suffer some organic brain disorder that causes him to be cantankerous. Maybe he never receives any favor or affection from his parents, or he's convinced that he's a failure, a worthless kid. (This is not to imply that children with these problems are necessarily disobedient and disrespectful.)

But there is another reason kids act like this. There are many children who are emotionally healthy, who receive liberal doses of favor and affection, who are growing in security, who have loving parents and a stable home environment, but who still act like this. Why? Because they haven't been trained to be obedient and respectful. It sounds too obvious, doesn't it? But obvious things are sometimes true!

In the next few chapters we will devote our attention to this task: training our young children to be obedient and respectful.

The Task Defined

Our task is to "train children to be obedient and respectful." The aim of the training we are considering is children who are obedient and respectful. Note that we are not treating many other important issues that require a training process. Why then the focus on training in obedience and respect?

First of all, obedience and respect is a priority from God's perspective. The only New Testament command directed specifically to children is, "Children, obey your parents" (e.g., Colossians 3:20). The chief command in the Old Testament directed toward children is the command to "honor your father and your mother."

Do You Love Obedience?

Our children have a way of reflecting in their behavior not only what they are taught explicitly, but also what they learn from us implicitly. Sometimes the attitudes we hold have an uncanny way of finding themselves reflected in our children. If we are honest with ourselves, most of us would have to admit that in our own hearts we do not honor obedience as much as God does. Our hearts can only change as we see who Jesus is and let his life transform our own.

What kind of a man was Jesus? He was an obedient man. At the age of twelve, Jesus and his parents had a little mis-understanding. The family was on a pilgrimage to Jerusalem. Mary and Joseph lost track of him. On their way back to Nazareth they realized that Jesus hadn't come along with the large group of relatives they were traveling with. The typical parental panic set in. Where is our boy? When Mary and Joseph found him back in the temple, they were naturally relieved and irritated with their son. How could you do this to us? Didn't you know we'd be worried about you? Jesus' response to their concern must have taken them up short, "Didn't you know I had to be in my Father's house?"

This is the first indication we have of what must have been an adjustment for Mary and Joseph. They had to come to terms with the identity and mission of their son—once a little boy, now becoming a man, and no ordinary man at that, but the Messiah, the Son of Man. Yet on this occasion, Luke records that after the discussion in the temple, "he [Jesus] went down to Nazareth with them and was obedient to them" (Lk 2:51).

Jesus was an obedient man. He was obedient to God and obedient to his earthly parents:

> During the days of Jesus' life on earth, he offered up prayers and petitions with loud cries and tears to the one who could save him from death, and he was heard because of his reverent submission. Although he was a son, he learned obedience from what he suffered and, once made perfect, he became the source of eternal salvation for all who obey him.... (Heb 5:7-9)

Jesus was an obedient man. He wasn't obedient "for the most part." He wasn't "sort of" obedient. He was perfectly obedient. Jesus was characteristically obedient. It wasn't simply something he could do from time to time; it was his characteristic response to godly authority. That is what we are aiming for in our children—not simply children who can be obedient and respectful from time to time when they are in the mood, but children who *are* obedient and respectful.

We love Jesus' mercy, his compassion, his power. We love his way of dealing with people, his way with words. We love his courage, his simple manliness. But do we love his obedience? Do we value his obedience? Do we want to be like him in his obedience? Do we see in his obedience the beauty of holiness, the purpose of God in designing man in his own image and likeness?

If we are thinking of obedience as merely necessary for the sake of maintaining a measure of order in the family, something that you have to have a little of in order to live in some kind of peace, we are missing the point. Obedience is a characteristic of the Son of God. We should learn to love obedience as we learn to love him. We should admire obedience as we admire him. We should value obedience to godly authority because we honor him who bears in his nature the stamp of the divine nature.

Many parents don't train their children to be obedient and

respectful because they don't really value obedience. Their training is half-hearted and double-minded. It lacks the power of conviction, and it just doesn't work that well. To train our children in obedience and respect, we have to submit our minds to the transforming influence of the mind of Christ so that we can "test and approve what God's will is." So this is the first reason for our focus on training children to be obedient and respectful: it is commanded by God and revealed in Christ.

But there is also a strategic reason for the focus on training young children to be obedient and respectful. As the proverb says, "Discipline your son while there is hope," implying that there is a time when training is most effective. The ripe time for training in obedience is the early years of a child's life. If a child can learn to obey his or her parents early on, so many other childrearing issues fall into place with less grief.

Formula for Success

To be honest, I'm a little bit suspicious of success formulas. I've never met a success formula that didn't seem to leave something out. But they are helpful for remembering certain key things. Here then is a formula for success in raising children to be obedient and respectful: a reasonably healthy home + clear standards for obedience and respect + consistent training in and enforcement of those standards = obedient and respectful children (more often than not).

The first part of the formula is beyond the scope of this book. By a "reasonably healthy home" I mean a stable home environment with mom and dad (if both are present) at peace with each other and at peace with the authorities in their own lives. There is love, favor, affection, general emotional well-being, and an adequate approach to limiting counter-productive influences from outside the family (a topic we will give some attention to later). I don't mean to imply that all these things must be working perfectly, or that it is not worth training in obedience and respect if there are substantial problems in any of these areas. They simply need to be recognized as an important part of the equation.

The second and third parts of the formula—clear standards of obedience and respect + consistent training in and enforcement of these standards—could be stated more simply. When Paul was writing to his assistant Timothy about Timothy's pastoral responsibilities, he told him to "command and teach these things" (1 Tm 4:11). Paul is speaking here not only of instruction but of instruction and enforcement. The Jerusalem Bible translation reads, "This is what you are to enforce in your teaching." Another way of saying it would be, "Teach and insist on these things." That's it in a nutshell: there are certain things we are to "teach and insist on" if we want to train our children to be obedient and respectful.

What to Teach and Insist on: Nine Rules for Children

If you want to insist on something with a child, you'd better be clear about what you're insisting on! That's precisely the purpose of the following nine rules for obedience and respect. Make them rules for your home and you will go a long way toward raising obedient and respectful children. If you are like me, you will feel that nine is an incomplete number. You will search your brain for that tenth rule, to feel that the list is complete. That's just as well because, in fact, the list *is* incomplete; it is suggestive, rather than exhaustive. Whenever appropriate, I've keyed the rules to the biblical view of love taught in 1 Corinthians 13:4-5. This passage provides an excellent text for teaching children.

> Love is patient, love is kind. It does not envy, it does not boast, it is not proud. It is not rude, it is not self-seeking, it is not easily angered, it keeps no record of wrongs.

1. Children should do whatever they are told to do, when they are told to do it, without fuss or resistance. (Love is not proud; it is not self-seeking.) Obedience isn't a mystery. It's doing what you're told. If we want to train our children to be obedient and respectful, we simply cannot allow them to refuse to do what we tell them to do. Every time we give a clear direction to a child and he refuses to do what he is told, and we allow him to get away with it, we are training him to say "no"—not to worldly passions but to godly authority.

Sometimes we parents have to give ourselves a little pep talk. We have to speak the truth to ourselves. We are in charge because God has put us in charge! We are parents, they are children! This is not our idea—a conspiracy of the bigger people to oppress the little people, a mere exercise in power politics. This is the way God planned it, the way he wants it to be for his glory and our good! This is not a time to be self-effacing or diffident. Our children need to understand the rules. We are responsible, under God, to teach our children his commands. Be explicit, clear, and unapologetic about this: "Children, you must obey your parents. That means you must do what Mom and I tell you to do."

To insist on this simply means that refusal should be unacceptable. Normally it should lead to punishment. (We'll talk more about the "how to" of punishment in the next chapter.) What is the difference between outright refusal (No! I won't!) and a response characterized by whining, complaining, ignoring the direction given? Not much. They are essentially the same response. Obedience means doing what you are told to do, when you are told to do it, without fuss or resistance. Many parents and others with responsibility to care for children tend to interpret refusal as inability. While it is a mistake to insist that a child do something which he is simply incapable of doing, many parents are so concerned about this that they err in the other direction. They are too quick to view a child's refusal as a sure sign of inability.

It is important, therefore, to learn what young children at the various stages of development (a two-year-old versus a four-year-old) are in fact able to do. For the most part, they are capable of greater obedience than many of us imagine. We'll treat this in greater depth in the next chapter.

2. Temper tantrums should not be allowed. (Love does not fly into a temper [Barclay translation].) What is a temper tantrum? These are the characteristic tantrum behaviors which are normally exhibited by a child when his or her will is being crossed:

—falling onto the floor in a heap
—rolling around
—screaming and yelling defiantly
—kicking things nearby
—defiant gestures (such as a clenched upraised fist)
—stamping of the feet

Temper tantrums seem to be like fingerprints; they are highly individualized with an infinite variety. Some children have a tightly controlled temper outburst (a distorted facial expression, clenched fists, and a stamp of the foot in response to a direction). Others are more expressive (the yellers and floor crashers).

There is room for children to express frustration and anger. If a child breaks a toy while he's playing with it and cries out, "Oh no!" while slapping his hand on the table, he doesn't need a stern rebuke. If his response is overboard, he'll need to be calmed down, but it doesn't need to be viewed as a temper tantrum. But children do need to learn that it is possible to go overboard with expressions of frustration. That is a line parents need to draw for their children. They especially need to learn that temper outbursts are not an acceptable response to direction from a parent or another responsible adult.

It is best to nip the temper tantrum syndrome in the bud. When you notice that your child is starting to have temper tantrums, teach him what a tantrum is and that it is not acceptable. It may take some specific role play to show him exactly what you mean by a temper outburst. At the next opportunity, provide a firm, assertive word of correction. If he doesn't respond to the verbal correction, provide a spanking to convince him that you mean business, especially when the temper outburst is a response to direction. Be level-headed and firm in your response. Don't let his excessive anger ignite your own.

It is possible for children to develop an emotional problem with anger which is rooted in some underlying psychological dynamics (for example, a child's anger may be a reflection of the unresolved anger of one parent toward his or her spouse). If this is the case, the normal approach of correction and discipline won't be as effective. In a few cases it may be counterproductive, but these are clearly the exception. The underlying problem will need to be addressed and some outside help will probably be needed. But it is also possible to develop an anger problem when limits are not set on anger reactions, or when children find that temper outbursts help them to get their way.

3. Children should obey parents and other trustworthy adults. In the Bible, obedience to God is expressed in obedience to parents, proper submission to governmental authorities, and proper submission to church leaders. To train a child to be obedient and respectful involves training him or her to obey adults who are trustworthy and have a legitimate role of authority. This might include teachers, babysitters, neighbors, brothers and sisters in the Lord, and relatives. We should make this very clear to children and back it up with discipline as needed. The child who disobeys a babysitter, for example, should have to answer to mom and dad.

Look for opportunities to reinforce the authority of trustworthy adults. Solicit reports from babysitters, child care workers, Sunday school teachers, and others who care for your child. Take the initiative to elicit information. Don't assume your child did fine. Many are reluctant to bring up a child's misbehavior—ask! How did Jo Anne do this morning with you? Did she obey you? Were there any problems?

If the child is old enough to connect delayed correction with the offense, provide the needed correction or punishment and have the child apologize to the caretaker. If the child is too young for this to be effective (he or she cannot make the connection between the offense and the consequences since too much time has elapsed), give the caretaker some specific guidelines for how to handle the misbehavior next time.

When you are a trustworthy adult and someone else's child misbehaves, report it to the parents. This applies especially when you share a common concern for raising children to be obedient with other parents. It is a responsibility—don't shirk it. Don't think of it as "ratting on a kid." It is for the good of the child. Besides, adults are in this together!

It can be helpful to give spanking privileges to the person who is caring for your child. This should only be done when you have confidence in the other person. If you do this, give the adult responsible details about how you administer a spanking so that consistency can be maintained. Let the child know that a given individual is authorized by you to give spankings when needed. Other disciplinary options can be passed on to those caring for your child as well.

It must be said that not all adults are trustworthy, and our children need to learn this. We should not foster a naive and indiscriminate acceptance of direction from all adults. Children need to be taught to be wary of strangers for safety's sake. They need to be warned of improper touching or sexual contact even from adults they know. They should never "keep a secret" from their parents, even if an adult tells them to. If something happens when mom and dad are not around that doesn't seem right, they need to tell their parents about it.

4. Children should not interrupt adult conversation. (Love is not rude.) My sister had some friends with a young child. She used to enjoy visiting her friends. I noticed that she hadn't done this in quite a while and asked her why. She replied, "Yes, it's a shame, but it just doesn't work. Their little girl won't let us relate." My sister is not the kind of person who is nervous around children or covers her furniture with plastic. But it seems common today for kids to interrupt adults repeatedly.

For young children, learning not to interrupt adult conversation or learning how to do so respectfully is a fairly sophisticated behavior. Especially in a society where respect for adults is not supported culturally, children need some focused instruction to learn the skill. It's a simple matter of teaching and insisting, but it requires some effort.

Teach: Make it clear what interrupting a conversation is. Act it out and say, "That's what interrupting is." Instruct the child on how to wait, how to gain your attention respectfully (for example, placing a hand on your leg and waiting for you to ask him what he wants to say), when to gain your attention respectfully, and when to wait. ("That's the sort of thing you should just wait to ask about until I'm finished. Off you go now.")

Insist: Correct the child each time he interrupts, and don't let it work for him to interrupt. Mark's dad corrected him every time Mark interrupted him. "Mark, don't interrupt me." But once he was interrupted and gave the correction, he proceeded to handle whatever Mark had on his agenda. "Where's Mom? Mom's at a meeting and will be back before bedtime." "You want a snack? Get some bread off the kitchen table." Dad's correction would have been more effective if he had said, "Mark, don't interrupt," then made Mark wait until he was ready to handle his concern.

If a child is not getting the idea through instruction and verbal correction alone, provide a negative consequence when he interrupts. Use the various forms of discipline in progressive levels of severity for training in this particular skill. Keep in mind that it does sometimes take a child a while to "catch on" to what is required of him.

5. Children should relate to the physical environment of adults with respect. (Love is not rude.) There is more to this rule than concern for keeping the furniture clean and intact. God reinforced the importance of fearing his name by requiring respect about things especially associated with his name. Remember Uzzah? He was an Israelite who accompanied the Ark of the Covenant on its journey back to Jerusalem during David's reign. The ark was the one object most closely associated with the name and the presence of God in Israel. Only certain men were authorized to touch the ark, and Uzzah was not one of them. When the ark began to tip over on the journey, Uzzah reached out to stabilize it. "The Lord's anger burned against Uzzah because of his irreverent act; therefore God struck him down and he died there beside the ark of God" (2 Sam 6:7). God was not concerned about getting fingerprints on the ark. He was concerned that his name be held in awe, regarded with fear, that his name be held up as holy. Likewise the Israelites were warned to treat the other objects associated with God—the temple and its furnishings, for example—as sacred items to treat with respect. Why? Because the objects are associated with God himself.

Obviously, the kind of respect children ought to show toward the things associated with adults is nowhere near the level of respect God required to be shown to the sacred objects associated with his name. The point of the example is simply to underline the fact that there is a connection between showing respect to a person and to objects associated with the person. If children are allowed to be loose around things associated with adults, they will take this as a cue to be disrespectful toward adults. Similarly if they are trained to treat "adult things" as adults do, they will be encouraged to treat adults with respect. Practically speaking this would mean things like:

—no standing on, jumping off furniture
—no playing with light switches
—no throwing books around

—generally, no abuse of furnishings and articles connected with the adult world

It is helpful if children can have some space which is their own turf—a portion of the basement, a playroom, or some other area in the house or apartment where they can handle things with a greater measure of abandon.

6. Children should not yell around adults who are engaged in adult activities. (Love is not rude.) Have you ever been sitting around in a living room, talking with some guests, while the kids are playing quietly nearby? Have you ever noticed how the decibel level tends to increase gradually until you find yourself shouting at the guests over the din?

What has happened? The children have become rude and disrespectful toward the adults. Children shouldn't yell or make disturbing commotions—what a range of activities that phrase covers!—around adults who are engaged in activities that don't call for yelling and commotion-making.

But kids are kids, and they need to play and let off steam. They can't just sit around like freshly scrubbed church mice! Of course! But they don't have to let off steam in the living room or near the porch where the adults are trying to have a conversation. Obviously this doesn't apply to situations where the adults are playing a game, roughhousing, and so on with the children. Then let 'er rip. Otherwise teach and insist that the children keep quiet or play elsewhere (often the simpler choice) if they are making too much noise.

7. Children shouldn't answer the phone until they've learned how to do so competently. (Love is not rude.) You are calling a friend who has a charming three-year-old son. After three rings you hear a "still small voice." Or is it merely some strange static on the line? Someone seems to be whispering something very gently, almost imperceptibly. Ahh! It must be Peter. "Peter, can I talk to your dad?" Silence. "Is your mom home?" "I love my Mommy" is the warm but irrelevant reply. "Could you please give the phone to Mommy or Daddy?" you ask, reduced to begging. Silence. Charmed but frustrated, you hang up the phone. When you pick it up again to redial, you can hear the breathing again. Then it dawns on you: you are at the mercy of this child. The irritation that some people feel when they ring up an answering machine is nothing compared with the sheer agony of trying to work through a three-year-old. Allowing little children to answer the phone before they can handle the responsibility is like asking your two-year-old to dish out the soup to the guests. A great thing to learn, dishing the soup out, but not that way.

8. Children should learn to greet adults. There are some modern maps of the Middle East which have a blank space in the area occupied by the state of Israel. These maps are produced by those who don't respect Israel's claim to be a sovereign state. One of the ways to withhold respect is to refuse to acknowledge another's presence. Have you ever noticed how commonplace it is for children in our culture simply to refuse to acknowledge the presence of other adults? Not a word, not a look, not a wave, nothing. This represents a loss of respect.

The skills of acknowledgement begin at an early age: looking mom and dad in the eye when speaking, learning to say hello, good morning, and good night. These things should be encouraged early on. They are not mere pleasantries. They foster respect for others. We should teach young children to say hello to adults, to learn their names when possible, and to stand up to greet them. Not a bad idea for us as well.

I live in a university town which follows only a few steps behind the "cult of the casual" found in places like southern California. When people here want to show a little respect they chew their gum more discreetly and try to keep the bubbles out of sight. Children are not encouraged to call adults Mr., Mrs., Miss, or Ms. I had an instructor at the University of Michigan who told us that he preferred to be called Mr. Eble, and we thought he was quite a character. I have a friend who called his father "Hank" instead of Dad. Nevertheless, we have our children refer to adults as Mr., Mrs., Miss, or, if they ask, Ms. Some adults act a little embarrassed or think my children are European, but most handle it quite well. I would recommend the practice as a simple and concrete expression of respect.

Especially in an environment where it is not widely practiced, greeting adults takes some practice. The families where I live whose children greet adults normally have to make a special point of teaching the kids how to do this. Practice at home, in the family first. If it helps, make it fun, a game that you play with your child to get him comfortable doing it. Begin to encourage very young children to say hello to adults, especially those they know well. When they do so, praise them. As they learn to greet adults, begin to insist that they greet others they don't know as well. Practice, teach, coach, give them more practice, and encourage them (remind kids just before guests arrive). Once you know they can do it, insist that they do it.

Don't apologize to a guest by saying "Jim is shy" when Jim fails to say hello. That tends to reinforce the notion in Jim's mind that he is subject to shyness (a form of social fear that can be overcome like any other fear). If he believes that he is shy, he will act shyly. Teaching, training, and insisting on can help a socially fearful child (and most children experience this at some point) to overcome the fear. This is a great service to the child as it will help him to be confident around new people.

If a child refuses to greet someone, and you know he is able to do it, a spanking may help him over the hump. I wouldn't suggest this until you've spent some time working with the child on the area. And there may be other forms of discipline that are equally effective, so there's no reason not to insist.

In the early efforts to train a child to greet adults, you may want to employ little rewards to encourage him. This provides a dual advantage: it helps the child to do it, and it convinces you that he is able, which allows you to confidently insist on the behavior later.

And remember, don't forget to greet people yourself!

9. Children should respect the dignity of others. (Love is kind.) Kids shouldn't get away with anti-social behavior: biting, kicking, abusive language, grabbing another child's toy. We should stress kindness in relating to other people, including other children. This applies to boys as well as girls. Sometimes parents excuse anti-social behavior in boys with the phrase, "Boys will be boys." True enough. But boys will also be mean and rude, and we shouldn't excuse that. Roughhousing and aggressive play can be great if it is mutual. However, unilateral bopping and shoving is just a euphemism for meanness.

Verbal forms of abuse are probably more harmful than physical forms. Name calling isn't kind, it's mean. It is worth outlawing more than obscenities. Calling other children "stupid" or "ugly," using slang put-down terms, even non-sensical names (you dingy-boo), should also be forbidden. In this area, we often apply a double standard to adults and children. We think that "just because they're kids," abusive language is something we can laugh away or hope they'll grow out of. Having a double standard for children in relating decently to other people only confuses them. There's simply no good reason for it.

Obedience Attitudes

As we establish rules for obedience and respect in our homes, it is helpful to keep in mind that we are aiming to foster certain attitudes in the children which support obedience and respect.

First of all, we shouldn't shy away from the fact that respect necessarily involves a measure of fear. Respectful children learn to "fear" their parents. What do I mean by this? In modern use, the term "respect" normally means one of two things. It either refers to a feeling of admiration like "I really respect you for that," or it is an acknowledgement of another person's rights like "I don't agree with your opinion, but I respect it," or "I respect your right to decide that." The word "fear" is hardly ever used in a positive sense. The biblical understanding is different.

The New Testament word translated "respect" in most modern translations is the Greek word *phobos*. In the older English translations, "fear" is used. The term is sometimes used in a negative sense, but often it is used in a positive sense. The term is sometimes used to describe the proper posture to take with those in authority over you. Just so, we are exhorted to fear God (1 Pt 2:17).

Why would the Bible use a word like "fear" to describe how we are to relate to God or those who exercise godly authority? Because there is a proper sense in which we ought to fear those in a position of authority. Part of what it means to respect someone is that we are disinclined to cross them. This doesn't mean that we are unable to cross them, or at times even supposed to cross them, but it means that our inclination is not to. For a child to develop respect for his parents means that it is not inwardly easy for him to disobey them. Something within him says, "I'd better do what I'm told or else things won't work well for me." Young children should not simply be willing to obey, but in some measure afraid not to obey.

When a child is properly respectful, when he has a healthy measure of fear, he doesn't need to be cajoled, persuaded, or tricked into obeying. If a child needs to be persuaded that a given direction from a parent is a good idea or wise or beneficial before he obeys the direction, he doesn't have the right attitude of respect or fear.

Certainly a child's fear toward his parents can be excessive or unhealthy. If a father is emotionally unstable or unable to control his anger, a child may be fearful of the father's emotions. Or a child may be in a state of apprehension about one of his parents, fearful and anxious about the relationship in the parent's presence. That is certainly not what we are aiming for. The problem many parents face in the present situation, however, is that there isn't a healthy measure of fear toward their authority. It's easy for children to disobey their parents, to flaunt their authority, to ignore it as simply irrelevant. Part of the reason for this is that parents have lost sight of the fact that there is a proper place for fear or respect in the relationship. Just as in our relationship to God proper fear and intimacy work hand in hand, the same is true for our relationship with our children. Closeness, intimacy, and a healthy fear of our authority are meant to work together.

There is a second obedience attitude to foster in our children. That is the attitude that obedience and respect are not a special virtue worthy of extraordinary reward. Obedience and respect are simply expected. They are a child's duty.

Jesus told a story to describe the attitude of a servant toward his service. The servant was out all day working in the fields. When he returned home, he didn't expect to get a break. He put on his cook's clothes and served his master dinner. He didn't expect a special reward for this because he understood that it was his duty. While it is helpful to commend children and praise them for obedience (and helpful in general to be liberal in our commendation of things well done), praise for obedience shouldn't be given in a way that suggests to the child that obedience is an extraordinary accomplishment, something over and above the call of duty. For example: "I know it wasn't easy for you to obey just now, but you did anyway— good for you, that's pleasing to God" is better than "You were an obedient girl today—what a wonderful girl, that deserves a special reward!"

Putting It into Practice: Obedience and Respect

> Remember the advice found in the Introduction on using this section. Use the exercises flexibly. Don't bite off more than you can chew. Better to focus on less and follow through than take a half-hearted stab at more.

1. Identify one of your children and complete the following inventory in light of his or her behavior.

Remember, most children in the modern world will have a long way to go before they are trained in these rules for obedience and respect. So again, welcome to the club.

- In the first column, place a check next to the rules you understand and agree with. Place a question mark next to the rules you don't understand or agree with.
- In the second column, evaluate your child's behavior using the following scale:

1 = Follows this rule most of the time, little training is needed.
2 = Follows this rule sometimes, more training is needed.
3 = Rarely follows this rule.

Understand/ Agree With?	Evaluating Child's Behavior	List of Rules
		1. Do whatever you are told, when you are told, etc.
		2. Temper tantrums are not allowed.
		3. Obey your parents and other trustworthy adults.
		4. Do not interrupt adult conversation.
		5. Treat the physical environment of adults with respect.
		6. Do not yell around adults involved in adult activities.
		7. Do not answer the phone until you have learned how to do it well.
		8. Greet adults when you see them.
		9. Respect the dignity of others.

NOTE: See the last page in this chapter for a list of these nine rules completely written out.

2. Of the nine rules, identify three that you would like to focus on over the next few months.

_____

_____

_____

3. Of the nine rules, select one that you would like to concentrate on first. Go ahead and pick one that looks easy. Note your choice below:

_____

For Group Discussion and Support

1. Report any steps forward you have taken in favor, affection, or confidence in the past weeks.

2. Discuss what is meant by a proper fear as an expression of respect.

3. Share one success you've had in implementing one of the rules for obedience and respect.

4. Share which of the rules seems most challenging to implement in your home.

5. Share any new insights you have about your own perspective on obedience and respect—a new understanding, something you hadn't taken into account before, some way that God is working to change your perspective.

6. End the session with group prayer. Thank God for any wisdom you have gained, for any steps forward you have taken in the areas studied thus far. Pray for help in specific matters as group members request it. Acknowledge any answered prayers from previous sessions.

Nine Rules for the Kids in the House

Here is a list of the nine rules mentioned in this chapter for handy reference. Feel free to cut it out and put it in a prominent place in your home.

1. Do whatever you are told, when you are told to do it, without fuss or resistance.

2. Temper tantrums are not allowed.

3. Obey your parents and other trustworthy adults.

4. Do not interrupt adult conversation.

5. Treat the physical environment of adults with respect. This means no jumping on furniture, no playing with light switches, no throwing of books, etc.

6. Do not yell around adults who are involved in adult activities.

7. Do not answer the phone until you've learned how to do it well.

8. Greet adults when you see them.

9. Respect the dignity of others. This means no biting, grabbing, kicking, or name calling.

FIVE

The First Two Years

I WAS OUT ON LONG LAKE with my daughter, Maja, who was fourteen years old at the time. As usual Maja was catching the fish. I was too busy putting on the worms and performing ear, nose, and throat surgery on small mouth bass who had swallowed hooks. At a certain point I realized that it was time for Maja to learn how to take the fish off the hooks. Maybe it was resentment over her good fortune, but I'd rather think it was my desire to teach her a new and important fishing skill. I don't know much about fishing, but one thing I do know is that there is no future in trying tentatively to hold onto a desperate fish. You have to grab hold of your slippery catch and you must do it firmly. Maja was not getting the hang of it. She would hold on to the fishing line (connected to the hook, connected to the fish's lip) like the caricature of a fine English gentleman holding a teacup. The other hand would make occasional forays near, but never quite onto, the fish itself.

Parents are often like that when it comes down to training their children to be obedient and respectful. Tentative. Uncertain. How easy it is to come to a firm conviction of the need for training in obedience, even to have a concrete vision for what obedient behavior is, only to flounder when it comes to putting it into practice with a particular child on a particular day in a particular situation. Train them to be obedient and respectful, yes! But how and when?

One of the reasons for being tentative is uncertainty about what level of obedience a child is able to learn at a given age. Is a one-year-old child able to be trained not to throw his or her food onto the floor? What about the "Terrible Twos"—is rebellion inevitable at that age? Is the objectionable behavior just a passing phase or something that needs to be addressed? What are the important obedience issues that require training for the three-year-old?

In the next two chapters, we will look at training in obedience and respect from a developmental perspective. We will walk through the process of training in obedience with a view to the nitty-gritty details present at different ages. Please keep in mind that the age categories are not hard and fast. Issues highlighted in one phase may well blend into another for one of your children. Individual children simply develop at different rates.

Elisabeth Elliot remembers her mother's advice: "By eighteen months of age, a child's will should be subject to his parents." Does that seem early to you? The noted missionary and author has revised her mother's timetable to two years. Most of us don't begin to think seriously about training the child in obedience until he's reached that age. Then we begin to notice that his will—which began as a very tender shoot springing out of the ground, like the crocus at Easter time—is now a clearly identifiable element of his personality. We no longer see his will as through a glass darkly, but we are seeing it in full view, face to face!

To say that a child's will is subject to the parents means that the child will yield to the direction of his parents when the child wants something else. The child will obey, submit, defer. In other words, by two years of age the basic power struggle should be settled. The parents are in charge, and the child has faced this fact and made his peace with it. This doesn't mean that the child is perfectly obedient by this time. It does mean that the basic issue has been settled—the child is at peace with being subject to his parents. His submission though will need to be reinforced and applied to his increasing maturity.

To say that a child's will is subject to his parents is not to say that he doesn't have a will. Far from it! His will is a gift from God, part of his personhood. Nor does it mean that his will is crushed or smothered. Instead, his will is subject to a higher authority, the authority of the parents.

Here again, we must remember that we are dealing with matters that touch a child's relationship to God. God is invisible to the child. The child's first encounter with God's authority is his encounter with the authority of mom and dad. It's not the only encounter with God's authority, but it is the first and its significance is not to be overlooked.

Remember, we are not just trying to get this little tyke to behave. We are not just trying to manage his behavior. We are not merely involved in a socialization process. We are dealing with basic and profound realities in the realm of the Spirit with this little child! He was not created to be independent of a higher authority. He was created with a will—with a power to choose, with an ability to have preferences and desires. But this will is meant to be yielded to God's authority. These issues go far deeper than concerns to have polite, sociable, cooperative children. These are issues at the very heart of God's relationship to human beings.

If Elisabeth Elliot is right—and all of my experience with my own children and the children of many others convinces me that she is—then training in obedience begins *before* the child's second birthday. Some of the choicest opportunities for training occur before the child reaches this age.

The First Nine Months

Remember that obnoxious dog I had who ate a whole avocado? He was a dog who lacked the basic desire to please his owners. I think I know what went wrong. We bought Lad from a family in crisis. The dog's owners were in a tizzy since the wife had just given birth to twins when her dog's litter arrived. Consequently, Lad was neglected. He wasn't held, petted, and played with by people. He hardly had any contact with human beings during the first six weeks of life. By the time we got him, Lad couldn't have cared less about people.

The first nine months of a child's life are a time for simply making personal contact with the child: meeting his needs for food, warmth, and comfort. It is a time for being affectionate. No, it's not much of a time for training in obedience, but it is a time when a foundation is laid for the child to develop an inclination to please his parents.

While it is not an active time for training in obedience, there are a few issues related to obedience that do come up. First of all, it is important to establish good eye contact with the child at this time. Look your child in the eye. This will prove to be important later on, when you are giving him or her direction.

Second, toward the end of this time in a child's life, he should begin to learn that there are limits to the demands he can make. For example, at a certain point some children will cry to be picked up at night just because they want to be held. They aren't hungry, their diapers are dry, their burps have been burped; they would just prefer to be held. That's fine except for the fact that a mom can become exhausted by a child who insists on being held two or three times a night. There is no hard and fast rule to this, but it is sometimes necessary to simply let a child "cry it out" once it is clear that there is no specific reason for his crying. As a child approaches the end of his first year, it is fine for him to begin to learn that not all of his demands can be immediately met.

Nine Months to Two Years

During these months, the child is progressively capable of receiving direction from mom and dad. He is beginning to develop a sense of self (he is able to differentiate himself from other objects) and a will (he begins to have various desires, wishes, wants that are beyond the basic biological needs). This is the time to begin training in obedience, so that from the very beginning his will develops within the context of a higher authority to which he defers.

There is a fairly predictable set of issues which come up during this time which provide occasions to train the child in obedience. These are times when a child's will needs to be crossed by yours. Think of these occasions as "obedience encounters" or "divine appointments"—occasions arranged by the providence of God to bring your child into a beginning understanding of obedience. (The phrase "obedience encounters" is borrowed and adapted from Alan R. Tippett and C. Peter Wagner, professors at Fuller Theological Seminary and leaders in evangelical renewal. They have spoken of "power encounters"—occasions when the kingdom of darkness is driven back by the power of God through healing or deliverance or some other action of God. Such encounters are inevitable and provide unique opportunities for extending the reign of God.)

Diaper-Change Time. During the early months, babies can be held still for diaper change quite easily. The job can be done peacefully. But as the child gets older—as early as nine to twelve months—one notices that the wriggling is more like that of a big-time wrestler trying to get out from under a move. We're not talking about wriggling caused by intestinal gas, but wriggling that simply indicates the child doesn't want to hold still. He or she is determined *not* to hold still.

At first mom meets this challenge with a firm voice, physical restraint, and a clear "Peter, be still." Remember Jesus addressing the wind and the waves! When it is clear that he has received the message yet is continuing to resist, follow up the firm voice with a light swat on the bare behind (or thigh if the bare behind isn't as bare as you had hoped). This simple encounter gets the message across: the child begins to understand that mom also has a will and it is unpleasant not to defer to her will.

Meal Time. At a certain point, the child sitting in a high chair will discover that meal time is, from his perspective, not only a wonderful time to express himself artistically in the "food medium," but also a convenient opportunity to develop his athletic abilities, especially his throwing arm. The moment your little artist becomes a Sandy Koufax is the moment you've been waiting for: an obedience encounter. When he begins to throw his food off the high chair, don't laugh, applaud, or ignore him. Establish eye contact and with a firm voice say, "Peter, no throwing food." Give verbal warnings a few times to guarantee that he has gotten the message. The next time he flings a brussel sprout, establish eye contact, give him a firm "no" and slap his hand.

Biting, hitting others, and doing dangerous things. These kinds of things like sticking one's fingers in electrical outlets or wandering into the street provide additional opportunities for training in obedience. Don't miss these opportunities. Drop whatever you are doing and engage your child in the training process. Take the time to deal with the situation, to see it through to conclusion. Accept the fact that obedience encounters never happen at convenient times. There is always something else going on at the time, and the last thing we want to deal with is a misbehaving child. For example, a friend of mine was getting into his car with two of his children. He had been over for a visit at my house, so I was escorting him to the car to see him off. His younger son, a toddler, was vigorously objecting to the fact that he had to sit in the back seat, even though it was his turn to sit in the back and he knew it. The typical whining and fussing ensued.

What do you do when something like this happens to you? When it's your toddler raising the ruckus? You're talking with your host, and it just isn't a convenient time to deal with a misbehaving child. What is the alternative to dropping what you are doing, in spite of the inconvenience, to engage in the training process when the opportunity presents itself? You can give in to Jimmy's demand and let him sit in the front seat. That will probably settle him down, restoring peace. Of course, then you still have the problem of what to do with Jimmy's brother who now believes, with good reason, that justice hasn't been done. It was *his* turn to sit in the front seat, but since Jimmy put up a fuss, he is sitting up there. Or, you can simply try to manage Jimmy's misbehavior. You physically stuff him into his toddler car seat while his fussing turns into shrieks of dismay. You manage a hasty and apologetic farewell to your host and speed off in the car. From the front seat you say different things to try to settle Jimmy down. First you try the firm approach, then you try to mollify him, and eventually you distract him by pointing out the accident up ahead. Halfway home, Jimmy finally settles down. What have you accomplished? Not much. The issue is over, peace has been restored, but what has Jimmy learned through the experience? He's learned that his behavior is an acceptable response to things not going his way. He's learned that you don't like his behavior, but he's also learned that it is acceptable. The next time his will is crossed, Jimmy will be more likely to respond in a similar way.

In order to train a child, you must be ready to engage him in the training process at any time, in spite of the inconvenience— to speak to him clearly, to observe his response to your direction, to take the necessary steps to insist that he obey you, to see the matter through to a successful conclusion. So instead of trying to smooth over the situation by trying to pay attention to the conversation with your friend and give some instruction to your misbehaving son, you drop what you're doing and see the training process through. "Excuse me, I've got something to deal with here," you say to your host. Then turning to your son, you gain his attention, look him in the eye, and say in a firm voice, "Now listen to me, Jimmy. It is your turn to sit in the back seat and that's the way its going to be. I want you to sit down and stop this fussing, right now—is that clear?" If Jimmy says, "Yes, Daddy," and sits down quietly in the back seat, you know you've made your point successfully. If his fussing continues, you know the training episode hasn't been concluded yet and you need to take further steps. Perhaps you ask your host if you can use his den to talk to your son privately. Then you take the child to the den and give him a spanking.

Once he's received the discipline, apologized to you for the misbehavior, and returned to the car where he sits quietly in the back seat, the issue has been settled.

Building a Better Vocabulary

To have a two-year-old who is subject to your authority, you will need to teach him or her the meaning of three words: no, yes, and come.

No. "No" is a much-maligned word in child-rearing circles. Parents of toddlers seem to feel guilty about using the word. When a cantankerous three-year-old says, "no" in defiance of the parent's direction, the knowledgeable observer is apt to say, "Well, it's no wonder—that's what he hears all day from his mom."

Sure it helps to eliminate unnecessary use of the term by "babyproofing" the environment, removing temptations, and so on. But with all that, you will still need to say "no" often. There's no reason to feel badly about it. "No" is a fine word, a useful word, a word that young children need to hear. It is one of the words whose meaning must be carefully guarded. Jesus said, "Let your 'Yes' be 'Yes' and your 'No,' 'No'" (Mt 5:37). This is great advice for parents. Don't say "no" unless you mean it. And when you say it, let it stand. Don't say "no" if you are not willing to follow it up and insist on it.

Remember that every time you say "no" without insisting on obedience, you are training the child to think that "no" is a complex term whose meaning differs according to the context. Sometimes it means stop immediately. Sometimes it means dad doesn't seem to like it, but he's not putting an end to it either. Sometimes it means "yes." This is not being gracious to the child. It is simply confusing to him.

Yes. As soon as the child is able to learn to say "yes," teach him to say "yes." Before that time, teach him to nod his head to indicate "yes." Then teach him to say or nod "yes" when you give him a direction. When you give a direction, as much as possible, insist on eye contact and insist that the child respond with a "yes." It may seem like a small issue, but in fact it is important for the child to have an explicit and concrete way of expressing his obedience.

Especially in young children there is a strong connection between the child's speech and his internal disposition. If the child hasn't been taught to express a respectful response to a direction, it will be more difficult for him to respectfully defer. On many occasions, the simple act of saying "yes" affects the internal act of complying with our directions. When a child is experiencing a strong disinclination to obey, the act of saying "Yes, Mom" functions as a key step toward actually obeying— it serves as a first step in the process of obeying, making it easier to actually complete the act of obedience.

The "yes" response is a way of measuring concretely whether a child has received a direction respectfully. This is especially helpful when the particular direction doesn't call for the child to do something immediately, and yet it is important for him to receive the direction respectfully. For example, instead of saying simply, "Julie, I don't want you to get food without asking me first," follow up the instruction with "Is that clear?" to elicit the "yes" response. If the child refuses to say "yes," you know that you have something to deal with.

Come. How many parents spend countless irritating and frustrating episodes chasing after a child who is in the "avoidance mode"? "Johnny, where are you? Come here, I'd like to speak with you." Johnny is not interested in hearing what you have to say, so he relocates. You follow him around and he picks up speed and throws in some fancy maneuvers. When you do catch up with him, he won't look at you, so you hold him gently by the arm and he begins to squirm away. You tighten your grip and he wails, "Anngh." Before you know it, a mini-scene is developing.

A great deal of this can be avoided when you make a point to train your children to understand what "come" means and insist that the word be obeyed at all times. When the child has learned how to get around (either as an accomplished crawler or a walker) begin to teach him what "come" means. Have him practice coming to you when you call him; commend him when he catches on. Then make it clear to him that whenever you say "come" you want him to come right away. Eventually begin to require obedience to this simple directive. Stick with it until he has the lesson learned. Once you know that he knows what is expected of him, and he refuses to do it, spank him if necessary.

Temper Tantrums

In the last chapter, we discussed what temper tantrums are and how to respond to them. It is quite likely that the child's first experiments with temper tantrums will occur sometime during his or her first eighteen months. A firm and even response at the first signs of temper outbursts during this phase will normally help the child learn the limits to his anger at a time when his anger isn't as powerful as it can become later on.

Watch Out for Denial

Many parents—especially with their first child—slip into a form of denial as their nine-month-old to eighteen-month-old begins to show early signs of willfulness and disobedience. It is just difficult to imagine that such an innocent, cute child would have the capacity for folly. But the proverb is true: "Folly *is* bound up in the heart of a child." Children do not automatically become obedient and respectful, knowing that it is pleasing to God. Left to their own devices, they are inclined in the opposite direction. True, children do have a strong inclination to please their parents, and this provides a powerful internal motivation for obedience. But for most children the inclination to please—a healthy thing in itself—isn't enough. They also need training.

The power struggle—who's in charge here—is inevitable and it begins early in life (before eighteen months). Parents need to be prepared to establish their authority during this period. Don't avoid the obedience encounters, welcome them. They are divinely appointed opportunities to train the child that God placed *under* your authority how to *respond to* your authority. There is certainly no need to create unnecessary encounters. In the normal course of life, there will be plenty to go around. But do welcome the ones that occur and seize the opportunity to do the training that leads to life.

As you are training your child, keep in mind those expressions of disobedience that will likely come up at a later date. Learn to recognize the early forms and be careful not to inadvertantly encourage behavior which is cute at twelve months but which will be a problem at twenty-eight months. It may be a real novelty when the one-year-old begins to say "no." But the parents who reinforce that with "oohs and ahhs" and other signs of delight are only making their job (and the child's) more difficult later on.

Establish an Effective Spanking Pattern

By the end of this first training period you should have established a good, clean, effective pattern for spankings. If you haven't spanked your child yet, it may be that you have an exceptional child. More likely, however, you've missed some helpful opportunities. An effective spanking includes the following elements:

1. Connect the spanking with the offense. The younger the child the more immediate the spanking needs to be. Tell the child what you are spanking him for. He may not be in a listening mood, so don't expect a dispassionate hearing from him and don't enter into a negotiation process. Simply inform him clearly: "You disobeyed me, didn't you? It's time for a spanking."

2. Have the child lean over your lap, or bend over a chair, or lie face down on the bed. As the child gets older, teach him how you want him to position himself to receive a spanking.

3. I recommend spanking on the bare bottom, using a smooth surface and fairly wide wooden object. I've found that "flyback" paddles work pretty well. (I'm referring to those wide wooden paddles with a ball attached by a length of elastic, the toy that was such a hit years ago. Of course, you'll have to remove the ball, the staple, and the elastic to transform your "flyback" into a paddle fit for spanking.) Your goal is to produce a non-injurious sting that will be enough to elicit a cry. How much force should you exert? Experiment on your own bare thigh to see what produces a sting without injury (no welts or bruising). One of the advantages of the paddle is the fact that you can produce a sting with less force than the bare hand. How many smacks with the paddle? I use six. Much less than that (one or two) is not likely to get the message across for most kids. A few more may be necessary for some. Obviously, spanking on the bare bottom is not appropriate beyond a certain age.

4. After the spanking, comfort the child for a little while as he settles down. Don't be apologetic. That can be extremely confusing to a child. Be matter of fact, firm, and loving. "Yes, I know that hurts, but you need to learn to obey... O.K. it's time to stop crying now."

5. Lead the child in repenting and asking you for forgiveness for the particular offense. This will vary according to his verbal skills and may only be a non-verbal exchange (hugging) until the child is able to say "Sorry, forgive me" or later, "I'm sorry for disobeying you. Please forgive me." As the child is able, insist that he express his apology and ask for forgiveness.

6. *Forgive the child explicitly in response.* "I forgive you, Tom." Give him a hug of reassurance and hold him on your lap for a time.

Sometimes parents, especially if they feel uncomfortable with spanking in the first place, will express their anxiety by being very lavish with their affection. They rock the child in their arms for an extended period, lavishing him or her with kisses and exuding sympathy. This can communicate insecurity and uncertainty on the parent's part and only confuses the child. Express simple, warm, reassuring affection, but don't overdo it.

In the context of forgiveness, it is often helpful to give instruction to the child, explaining more about what should change in his behavior, the reason it is not acceptable, and how to handle things next time. If he was spanked for refusing to do something he was told to do, have him do it now.

This should bring closure to the discipline. Relate to the child as if he has been forgiven. Don't express residual anger toward him. Don't be cool and aloof.

During these months when you are establishing your authority with the child and he is beginning to receive physical discipline, *remember to be generous with favor and affection as you relate to the child throughout the day*. This will help to reassure him that your discipline is consistent with your love for him and will provide added security to receive the discipline that is needed.

Putting It into Practice: The First Two Years

1. Think about how eye contact works between you and your young child.

- Do you look 'em in the eye?
- Does he or she look you in the eye?

In the next day or two, make a special point to establish good eye contact with your children. Put a few "Look 'em in the eye" signs around the house if you need a reminder.

2. Think about how physical punishment works in your home. If you have given spankings to your children, list the steps involved. (First I tell him what he did wrong, then I put him over my knee, and so on.) List what you normally do—not what you think you should do.

* _____

* _____

* _____

* _____

* _____

Compare your present pattern with the steps outlined in the chapter. Make a new list of steps. Include any changes you would like to make in your routine for spanking.

* _____

* _____

* _____

* _____

* _____

3. If you have a child who is between one and two years old, list three obedience issues that you would like to help him or her with over the next year.

(1)_____

(2)_____

(3)_____

For Group Discussion and Support

1. If you have a child in this age group, share with the group your impressions about the key obedience and respect issues you are facing.

2. Share your personal background on the matter of physical punishment. Is there anything in your experience that makes you concerned about how it is handled? Is it difficult for you to administer a spanking?

3. Share the single piece of advice from the chapter that you think would be of most help in your situation.

4. Pray together for God to grant wisdom and help for the specific challenges mentioned by members of the group. Intercede for the specific children in the families that are in your group.

SIX

Beyond Toddlerhood

T O SAY THAT BY TWO YEARS a child's will should be subject to his parents might imply that the job of training in obedience and respect is finished before the child has reached his second year. If only it were that easy! In fact, it only means the child is in a position to get on with the training that he will increasingly be in a position to receive as he matures. So don't give up yet. God is with us, and there's a great deal more to be done!

Eighteen or Twenty-four Months to Three Years

During the time between eighteen months and three years some pretty interesting things are happening with this young child. One day you will wake up and say to yourself, "Wow! This kid is changing. Where did he get that strong will?" Remember the farmer in Jesus' parable about the crop that grew while he slept? He woke up after a good night's sleep and wondered at the sight of his crop coming up. I don't know how it happened or exactly when, he thought. I don't remember doing anything to speed it along its way; it just grew!

Your child is developing a much more defined sense of self. And his will is developing at the same time. His likes and dislikes are more defined. He's beginning to develop opinions about more things, more "likes" and "dislikes." The goal of training during this time is not to quench the development of his will but to continue to channel its growth within the context of submission to a higher authority (the authority of his parents, commissioned and authorized by God). As his will grows, he needs to learn how to submit it so that it doesn't run wild.

Are You Up to the Test?

This is also a time of testing. The child is testing you. He wants to know whether or not you will continue to insist on obedience, in light of the fact that he feels more strongly about things than he did before. Maybe you weren't all that serious earlier on! He is physically, emotionally, and mentally more capable of disobeying you. Are you still physically, emotionally, and mentally equipped to secure his obedience?

Many refer to this time in a child's life as "the Terrible Twos." Sometimes those who use the phrase give the impression that little can be done to get a two-year-old child to behave—the only hope is to ride out the storm. Most of us can readily picture the typical scene. The parent of a misbehaving two-year-old smiles sheepishly at a stranger passing by on the sidewalk. The stranger steps around the child who is stamping his feet and yelling, "I don't want to come home!" Clearly embarrassed, the parent explains, "The Terrible Twos!" The sympathetic stranger then replies knowingly, "Ah yes! The Terrible Twos." Ask a two-year-old child to behave himself? It's like asking someone with a cold not to sneeze!

It is my opinion that we would be better off to drop the phrase "the Terrible Twos" from our everyday vocabulary. First of all, the phrase itself encourages the view that terrible behavior is normal during this time and that little can be done except to "ride out the storm." It is normal for the two-year-old child to test the limits during this time, but there is no reason to expect terrible behavior as the inevitable norm. It is actually possible to train your child to be an obedient and respectful two-year-old.

The term "the Terrible Twos" as a description of this phase of development can function as a self-fulfilling prophecy. It can suggest to the child that he is expected to be terrible during this time. Often he is all too willing to live up to the expectation. In fact, the prevalence of the term is merely symptomatic of the fact that many parents have lost a vision for the role of training in raising young children. They have lost sight of the importance of training in obedience and respect at an early age.

What are the key issues of obedience and respect for the year-and-a-half to three-year-old child?

This is the time when the rules for obedience and respect referred to in Chapter Four become a major focus of training. The nine rules represent a simple and manageable set of rules for the child to begin to master through these months. You may have a few more to add to the list in your home, but for the most part these nine will cover a great deal of ground in training your child to be obedient and respectful. The foundation for observing many of the rules will already have been established before this time. But this phase of development is the time for making the rules very clear and enforcing them consistently.

As the opportunities arise for establishing and enforcing the rules, make a point to express each rule clearly, drawing attention to the specific behavior you are concerned with. Keep the expression of the rule simple, consistent, and memorable. For example, if your two-year-old child is jumping on the furniture, don't just say, "Don't do that." Take the opportunity to make the rule clear: "Jill, there is no jumping on furniture in this house. Stop it please." Use of the same phrase at each occurrence ("No jumping on furniture in this house" or something equivalent) makes the rule more concrete and memorable for the child.

When obedience is the issue, make it explicit. Don't say to a child who is disobedient, "Cut that out!" or "I don't like the way you are responding to me!" Children think in very concrete terms. General or vague statements of displeasure or disapproval may not effectively draw their attention to the behavior you are correcting. Be specific and point out the obedience issue. "You didn't come here when I told you to. That's disobedience. But you know that you must obey me."

The only way to establish the rules for obedience and respect and to train your children to obey them is to consistently enforce them. Once you have laid down the rule, aim to deal with every infraction in order to let the child know that you mean business. In the ebb and flow of everyday life this may not in fact be possible. There will be times when through weariness or inattention, or even simple sensory overload, you will miss opportunities to enforce the rules. Some children will capitalize on these lapses in consistency more than others. But for all children, a reasonably consistent enforcement is required to secure obedience.

Speech

Children begin to blossom as talkers between the age of eighteen months and three years. Most parents are mightily impressed, and why not? The capacity to speak is no small achievement—a reflection of the fact that we are created in the image of God. In fact, it's easy for parents to become so enamored by the wonder of it all that they unwittingly encourage the child to jabber constantly without learning the place of restraint in speech.

Our third child, Amy, was born six years after her older sister. We forgot some of the things we should have remembered from raising her older siblings. When Amy began to talk we were delighted. Before long our daughter's verbal skills gained more influence in the family than we had bargained for. She began to rule the dinner conversation with her chatter. Finally, we realized that we had neglected to temper our initial enthusiasm for the emergence of speech with the biblical perspective on the tongue, especially the exhortation to restrained speech. "When words are many, sin is not absent, / but he who holds his tongue is wise" (Prv 10:19).

We weren't teaching Amy how to hold her tongue. She needed our help to learn. Slowly but surely we began to establish boundaries for her speech. For a while, I had Amy sit next to me during dinner so that I could give her more concentrated instruction. At times I would simply tell her to listen without saying anything for a period of time. Sometimes a hand on the shoulder and a signal to be quiet helped. We began to teach her simple things like, "When a guest walks in the door, don't start telling him what you did today. Say hello first, then let him get settled. Wait your turn."

It is also important from the earliest emergence of speech to insist on respectful speech. Insist on kind speech about and toward others. It is very common among young children to hear a good deal of mean-spirited speech—calling others by derogatory names and making fun of weaknesses, for example. Parents sometimes let this go on with the thought: "They don't really know what they are saying," or "That's just the way kids are." But speech of this kind simply shouldn't be tolerated.

Sharing

During the early months of this period, the child is learning the concept of ownership. He or she is learning what "mine" means. This is a normal and necessary part of the child's development. So it is good for him to have some things that he can relate to as "mine," things that for the most part he controls under parental supervision. As he is learning that some things are "mine," the child should also be encouraged to learn to share what he has with others. When, on what may seem like the rare occasion, the child spontaneously shares something, commend him for it on the spot. Teach him what it means to share. Encourage him to share. There will be some situations when it will be appropriate to insist that he share some of his things with others.

Bedtime

Ah bedtime! Speech and learning to share are all well and good, but now he's getting down to brass tacks, you say.

Bedtimes have the potential to be precious times with young children. Read them a Bible story, give another brilliant answer to yet another question about the Trinity, shower them with hugs and kisses, spend a time of prayer, and then it's off to never-neverland for the tired youngster. And it's time for a little peace and quiet for mom and dad. Unless, of course, the child hasn't yet learned that mom and dad are in charge. Then bedtime is altogether a different scene. Ask the weary (and just a bit discouraged) parents of a young child when bedtime occurs and you might well elicit a cynical chuckle. "Bedtime for Bobby? Between eight and eleven P.M. We start at eight and he eventually wears down by eleven."

Young children will test the bedtime limits you set with incredible endurance, and they often need to learn the obedience lessons in this arena before bedtimes can be peaceful for all concerned. What can you do if your three-year-old child refuses to go to bed, or spends the hour after being "tucked in" jumping on the bed, or comes out for drinks of water every fifteen minutes, and so on?

First of all, do all the common sense things to make bedtime easier for you and the child. Reserve thirty minutes or even an hour before bedtime for quieter activities. Don't wrestle with your kids five minutes before bedtime and expect them to "switch off." See that they have had plenty of tiring physical activity during the day, including after the afternoon nap. Avoid food and beverages that tend to charge them up.

Second, settle on a reasonable hour for the actual bedtime. Consider all that needs to happen before the lights are out (will you need fifteen minutes or half an hour?), and consistently begin the process at that time.

Develop a consistent bedtime ritual. For example:

The Call to Bedtime: "Time to Get Ready for Bed Now"
The Collection of the Toys
The Cleansing of the Teeth (and related duties)
The Procession to the Bedroom
The Reading of the Bible Story
The Reflections on the Day
Closing Prayer
Benediction
Recessional of Parent from Bedroom

As much as possible, stick to the order of service and let the child know what comes next. Until it is established as a pattern, be prepared to lead him or her through each step. That will require setting aside the necessary time to do the training rather than trying to do a lot of other things at the same time. In other words, supervise him closely for a time, step by step.

For each step, gain his attention, look him in the eye, give a clear and simple direction (time to get ready for bed now, time to brush your teeth, etc.), and elicit the "Yes, Mom" or "Yes, Dad" response.

At a time other than bedtime, sit down with the child and lay out some basic rules and expectations for the ritual. Make it clear what you expect from him. Let him know that when you inform him that it's time to start getting ready for bed, you expect an obedient response: "Yes, Mom." Discussion and negotiation won't result in a later bedtime (this is especially important during the period when you are training the child in going to bed without resistance and fuss). Let him know that if he doesn't do what he's told, there will be consequences. For example, if your child is informed that it's time to get ready for bed and he throws a temper tantrum, he'll get a spanking. If he's disobedient he will be punished. It may be helpful to include a reward for cooperative behavior. For example, if he responds positively, he'll have an extra story read to him.

When you begin to implement the process, remind him again of what is expected.

Getting children to bed peacefully and obediently is only half the battle. You will also need to decide on what you will allow once they've been tucked in. Take care of all the standard distractions and reasons for getting out of bed before turning out the lights (the drink of water, finding the favorite blanket or stuffed animal, going to the bathroom, and so on).

Some children can handle being allowed to sing or talk quietly with a sibling for twenty minutes, with a reminder from a parent to be quiet after the time is up. Other children will only be tempted to become more and more active if the line isn't more clearly drawn. You may decide to allow one occasion for getting out of bed to use the bathroom or none, depending on what seems best. At any rate, make the rules simple and clear. Remind your child what the rules are until the training is finished. Decide on the consequences for disobeying the rules and consistently enforce them.

Some children can learn this process without a great deal of effort on your part. But other children will require a period of concerted attention. It may be necessary to have one parent free from 7:30-9:00 P.M. for a week or two to engage in the training process as the top priority during that time. Make sure a parent is available. That means keeping the phone off the hook and being free from all other activities so you can really attend to the training. Normally, the time invested in clearly thought out and focused training over bedtime is well worth it in the long run.

Toilet Training

While I'm no expert on the various techniques of toilet training, I would urge parents not to approach toilet training as a matter of obedience, if at all possible. Certain aspects of toilet training may inevitably include an obedience issue, but for the most part it is not the best issue to handle as primarily a matter of obedience.

Why not? First of all, it is sometimes difficult to judge the child's actual ability to control bowel and bladder, especially in the earlier phase of toilet training. Children develop the physiological capacity to control bowel and bladder at different rates. If you require something the child is not physiologically capable of, you're only inviting frustration.

Second, the issue has a high degree of emotional content. The issue is more than a simple functional process. It is also related to matters like a child's body image. It is easy for the child to experience a strong sense of shame connected with failure. Raising the issue to a matter of obedience often simply adds a level of intensity to the whole process that is not helpful.

Handling Stubborn Responses to Spanking

Young children who are prone to be especially stubborn, who are energetically testing the limits, may go through a time of fighting against a spanking. They may respond angrily, yell, refuse to hold still or be held still for the spanking, or simply refuse to yield to the parent's authority.

When I first began to use physical punishment with my son Jesse, he wasn't at all used to the idea. He was used to disobeying without effective consequences. During one of his first spankings, (he was about four years old at the time) he responded with stubborn anger. Nothing was going to make him say he was sorry for disobeying. I told him that if he didn't receive his discipline and apologize for disobeying, he would be spanked again. He received a few spankings in a row before he gave in. That was a turning point in his response to authority.

What's a parent to do?

First of all, apart from an actual punishment episode, talk things over with the child according to his age. Give him some instruction on the role of spankings and how you want him to respond. Give him very concrete instructions about how to receive a spanking, (lean over the bed/my lap like this and put your hands here). Let him know that crying is fine, but yelling in anger is not. Show him what fighting back is and tell him it isn't acceptable. The next time he fights back during a spanking, warn him. If he doesn't stop, treat the fighting back as a separate act of disobedience and give him a second spanking. When he does respond better to punishment, commend him for it.

A few words of caution are necessary here. First, make sure that you are not losing control through your own frustration or anger. That can be very frightening to a child and will create a bigger problem than the one you were originally trying to address. If you have any concerns about this, it is time to get some perspective from someone you respect and trust.

Second, there's obviously a limit to how often you can spank a child. If the child has lost control or the ability to respond (as contrasted with maintaining a stubborn posture), another approach is necessary.

Third, if a child is dealing with a more serious emotional problem or a learning disability, he or she may not be able to respond. There may be something else besides garden-variety stubbornness fueling his response. He may be affected by a strong insecurity or fear. He may be affected by some unresolved anger working in the family. Again, getting some outside help from a respected and trusted source can help you in sorting through the problem.

Dealing with Disobedience through Distraction

Many child-rearing experts, especially in the last twenty years or so, recommend a heavy dose of distraction as the prime way of dealing with disobedience in a toddler. Distraction does have a place, especially as a means to help a child from getting into trouble in the first place. For example, if your two-year-old child is characteristically cranky after waking up from a nap, you may want to put special effort into giving him something focused to do rather than leave him to his own devices during this emotionally vulnerable time. But distraction can be an obstacle to training a child when a parent distracts a child rather than responds directly and straightforwardly to the child's disobedience.

If you say to your two-year-old child, "Stop yelling please" and he responds with a bold "no," or if he simply refuses to heed your direction, your authority is being tested. You must deal with the matter head on. To buy a measure of peace by responding to his refusal with, "Come on Ronnie, I'll put a record on for you," is a mistake. When a child is doing something that he shouldn't be doing, parents ought to expect that the child can learn to respond to a simple and direct form of correction. Relying on distraction at those times merely avoids the obedience issue and reinforces the child's view that obedience isn't really required.

Note to Fathers

Often mothers are the ones to spend the most time with small children—and that usually means they carry the load of discipline. Fathers can do a few things to support their wives during this trying time. First of all, dads can make a point to stay informed about what has been happening with the kids during their absence. Second, dads can take the primary responsibility for providing discipline when they are home, to help balance the sheer workload that discipline represents. Third, fathers can make a special point to reinforce the wife's authority in the eyes of the children. If a child disobeys his mother in your presence, step in and correct the child, "That's no way to respond to your mother. Now you do what you were told right now." Sometimes moms can get worn down by children at this age. The father's vigor in dealing with disobedience can be a great support.

If a child speaks disrespectfully toward mom, the father

should respond with a special measure of gravity. "You said *what* to your mother? Who do you think you are, young lady—that's your mother you're talking to."

My father insisted that we express respect toward our mother by always referring to my mother as "Mom" rather than "she" or "her," whether Mom was present or not. I've found it a helpful way to reinforce the respect that my kids have toward their mother.

Three Years to Six Years

After the child has passed through a time of testing your commitment to obedience and respect, he or she may enter a period of what looks (by comparison) like uncanny cooperativeness. Be thankful; training in obedience works over time. But don't assume that obedience and respect are issues of a bygone era. If a child is left to his own devices, he is quite capable of regressing.

Training in obedience and respect should continue during this time. Two additional issues are likely to surface that will require your attention: the emergence of "why?" and lying.

Why. The watchword of the older school-age child (by my small sampling, especially the boys) is "fine."

How are you doing today, son?

Fine.

How was school?

Fine.

How about gym class?

Fine.

What's your favorite grade of sandpaper?

Fine.

The watchword of the inquisitive three-year-old and four-year-old child is no doubt, "Why?"

That is a pretty red bird, isn't it?

Why?

That ball really bounces high.

Why?

Time for bed now.

Why?

The emergence of this new watchword is often met with great enthusiasm, and rightly so for it indicates a healthy and normal curiosity. The child is interested in things. But it is important for parents to discern the "why" which is a genuine expression of curiosity from the "why" which is a tool to resist parental direction.

The former should be met with patient explanation where time and understanding permit. (I've often had plenty of patience but little understanding. Why *is* an egg yoke yellow?) But parents should not think that every "why" in response to direction should be satisfied. Often when a child responds to a simple direction with, "But why?" he is merely indicating that he doesn't like the idea. This is especially clear when the directions are part of the normal routine. The parent says, "Time for bed now," or "Brush your teeth after breakfast." The tone of voice makes it clear that the "why" is not an expression of academic curiosity. That kind of response should be discouraged and replaced with the simple "yes" of obedience.

When a direction is out of the ordinary, a child may sincerely wonder about the reasons. The child's tone of voice isn't whining or defiant. He doesn't give the impression that his obedience is contingent on your response. The reasons for the direction in this case can be explained. But this shouldn't lead to a prolonged process of negotiation, which soon becomes a tug of war between parent and child. For younger children, it is perfectly appropriate, when faced with a "why" in response to a simple direction to say, "Do it first, and then I'll explain the reasons if you are still interested."

Lying. It is quite common for lying to surface at this time. Don't be shocked. Most kids at least experiment with lying a few times. How should a parent deal with lying?

1. Don't lie to the child, not even so called "white" or innocent lies. It is my opinion that it is a mistake to deceive children about figures like Santa Claus and the tooth fairy. If you want to have fun with these figures, children are quite capable of enjoying them as pretend characters. Little children will have a difficult time knowing what is play and what is real. That's fine, as long as parents don't hide the fact that it is all a game. But as soon as children become capable of distinguishing fantasy and reality, they are moral rigorists who do not appreciate shades of gray. It isn't helpful for them to discover that Santa Claus doesn't really exist, that they have been duped all along. That just sends confusing signals about the legitimacy of deception.

Also be careful not to lie to other people. Children can easily pick up on forms of lying that may seem socially acceptable, like calling in "sick" when you are only sick of work. Or telling a friend you can't come over because you are having guests, when you are not having guests at all but only searching for an easy out. Let the child see you telling the truth or dealing honestly even when it is inconvenient. If the check-out lady undercharges you for an item, bring it to her attention. Explain to the child what you did and why.

2. Help the child to distinguish between what is real and imagined. The line between the two can be surprisingly thin for children. Keep this in mind and don't be too quick to accuse the child of lying in the early going.

3. Teach your children what lying is—give illustrations, point out examples in stories, and so on. Teach him that lying is wrong, that "an honest answer / is like a kiss on the lips" (Prv 24:26). Teach him that God wants us to "speak the truth in love," that it pleases God when we tell the truth even when it isn't easy to do so.

4. When you first discover that he is not telling the truth, use the occasion as a teaching opportunity. Sometimes you may only strongly suspect that a child is lying. That may be a sign that it's time to do some more teaching (apart from the incident at hand) as well as time to keep your eyes open for a more clear-cut case of lying, an occasion when you can demonstrate that he was lying. The latter occasions are much more effective for correcting the child. Use the first one or two occasions of clear-cut lying to correct the child firmly, without using physical punishment.

In the meantime, give the child opportunities to be truthful when it is inconvenient, and commend him for it.

5. If lying persists after an initial period of instruction and correction, don't let him get away with it. If the case is clear cut, give him a spanking to let him know that lying is not acceptable.

Recurrent or habitual lying that doesn't respond to these measures over time probably requires a closer look.

Engaging the Heart

As the child matures, it is increasingly important to engage his heart—that is, to build an open and positive relationship. "Win" the child even as you are training him.

Remember to express an appropriate measure of honor toward the child. He is a child of God and he should be treated as one worthy of honor. In the press and irritation of everyday life, it is easy to slip into a drill sergeant style of communication with the kids. But there is every reason to combine a firm, straightforward approach to giving directions with a graciousness that respects the child's dignity. Observe the normal conventions of gracious communication, such as "please" and "thank you." Listen to the child when he is speaking and draw him into conversation. Be very careful not to slide into even mild forms of ridicule or mockery.

One of your goals during this time is to help the child to

freely disclose himself to you. This is not something to push (a lot of four-year-old children don't have a great deal to disclose yet) but to foster. Make a point to draw the child into conversation. Especially as he spends more time outside the home, teach him how to share the simple details of what he did during the day.

Bedtime seems to be one of the best times for engaging in this kind of personal conversation. Capitalize on the trace of tiredness, the natural desire to stay up as long as possible, and the lowering of defenses that bedtime can bring. Review the day, ask questions, be available to answer questions, talk about the Lord. Bedtime stories provide a natural time for talking things over.

Open communication will become an increasingly important channel for teaching and training, for shaping the child's conscience, and for influencing his values. It is also part of the process of winning a child's heart so that he wants to identify with his parents. Winning his respect by managing his unruly impulses through firm limits and discipline is part of this process, but there is also a kind of "wooing" that takes place as well.

Another way to develop this dimension of the relationship with children is to begin the practice of taking "special times" with mom or dad. In our family, a "special time" is when Nancy or I take one of the kids out for some time alone. For the younger kids, we make a point of referring to it as a "special time." It might mean a half-hour at a local park, or a trip to a fast-food restaurant for lunch, or combining a trip to the hardware store with a visit to the ice cream parlor. It's a time for paying attention to the child, talking, asking questions, expressing favor, or doing some instruction or encouragement. Frequency may vary according to the time available, the number of children, and their ages and needs. Whether it's weekly or monthly or "every now and then," it is a time to make it clear that you want to do something with the child because you enjoy his or her company. You communicate to him that the relationship is important to you.

Putting It into Practice: Beyond Toddlerhood

1. How does your child handle speech during the dinnertime?

• Does he or she interrupt others frequently?

• Has he learned how to ask politely for what he wants?

• Is he dominating the dinnertime conversation?

Focus on training your child in speech during the dinnertime. Make a list of three simple objectives or rules to teach and insist on:

(1) _____

(2)_____

(3)_____

This week focus your training on one of these objectives. Teach him what you expect. Remind him at the beginning of each meal. Correct him as needed. Commend him for improvement. Decide what punishment, if any, you will use as part of the training process. Move on to the next objective when the first has been mastered.

2. Review the bedtime ritual in this chapter. Write down an "order of service" for bedtime to suit one or more of your children.

• _____

• _____

• _____

• _____

- _____

- _____

- _____

- _____

- _____

Every night for a week or two, review the order of service and what is expected for each step in the process. Teach, insist, commend, correct, and punish disobedience once your expectations are clear.

3. Consider the role both you and your spouse have in disciplining your small child. Do both of you share the load of discipline, or is it left largely for mom to shoulder? How can the load be shared more equally by both of you? Note any decisions you make together in the space provided.

_____

_____

_____

_____

For Group Discussion and Support

1. By now, everyone in the group could use a little encouragement. Select a third of the group's members as targets of an encouragement campaign.

- Pass around a sheet of paper with the targeted person's name at the top. (One sheet per person to be encouraged.)

• The other group members should jot down one thing they admire about the person related to his or her role as a parent.

• At the end of the meeting, give the paper to the person selected for encouragement.

Do this at the next two group sessions until everyone has been commended for their strong points.

2. Discuss how bedtime works at your house. Share what works well and what could stand improvement.

3. What have you learned about teaching your young child to share with others?

4. Share any progress you've made in establishing one of the nine rules for obedience and respect with your children.

5. Close with prayer together.

SEVEN

Winning the War
on Whining

WHEN I FIRST MENTIONED this chapter title ("Winning the War on Whining") as the title of a talk I was giving to a group of about four hundred parents, a spontaneous cheer erupted. I could only guess that either a lot of us had friends and relatives seeking advice on how to handle *their* whining children, or we were facing our own whining kids back home. I have a hunch it was the latter because in that brief moment, you could feel something in the atmosphere of that auditorium. We were not just isolated parents, struggling along. We were an oppressed people, who had found solidarity in a common cause: winning the war on whining.

What is whining? *Whine: 1. to utter a low, usually nasal complaining cry or sound, as from uneasiness, discontent, peevishness, etc. 2. to snivel or complain in a peevish, self-pitying way.* That's what it says in the unabridged edition of *The Random House Dictionary of the English Language.* This definition is truly inspired, but Webster's more accurately describes whining as a high-pitched sound. For our purposes, we could expand just a bit on these dictionary definitions with the whining of young children in view. *Whine: A response characterized by dissatisfaction, complaint, bargaining, resistance to direction, and ex-*

pressed through tone of voice and facial expression. Often it is a form of disrespect. It should be contrasted with open defiance on the one hand and cheerful obedience on the other.

Bedtime at the Smilovitz's . . .

DAD: Time for bed, Princess.

JENNY: (a touch of dismay, mingled with a sense of injured justice) Bed?

DAD: That's right—time for bed now.

JENNY: (tongue clicks in disappointment, face contorts in an expression of pain) Oh no, not bed, not now!

DAD: (with growing aggravation) That's right, now.

JENNY: But what about Charlie? He doesn't go to bed until nine o'clock.

DAD: Charlie is also two years older than you are.

JENNY: It's not fair. Why do I have to go to bed so early? None of the other kids do. I'm the only one in the whole world who goes to bed this early.

DAD: Come on, let's move it.

JENNY: (sighs and rolls eyes) Dad!

Dinnertime at the Montgomery's

MOM: What kind of dressing would you like on your salad, Julie?

JULIE: What is there?

MOM: Thousand Island and Ranch.

JULIE: No French?

MOM: No French.

JULIE: (just a hint of a pout) I'll take Thousand Island, I guess—but the lumps are creepy.

MOM: (as she passes the dressing, mom inspects the bottle more closely) Julie, I'm afraid it's almost gone.

JULIE: But I wanted Thousand Island!

MOM: I thought you said it was creepy.

JULIE: I said the *lumps* are creepy . . .

MOM: I'll get some Italian from the kitchen.

JULIE: It's greasy! It slides down my throat. It makes me choke. (plaintively) Mom!

MOM: Julie, don't "mo-om" me. (Mom imitates Julie's pronunciation of "mom" which includes at least three extra syllables for emphasis.)

JULIE: I want Thousand Island, I need it.

MOM: (turning to her husband, Tom, with a hint of pleading desperation) Tom, these kids . . .

What's Wrong with Whining Anyway?

Surely whining in young children is irritating. Certainly it adversely affects the atmosphere at home. Lots of things are irritating but are not obedience issues in training our children. So what's wrong with whining?

> So then, my beloved, just as you have always obeyed, not as in my presence only, but now much more in my absence, work out your salvation with fear and trembling; for it is God who is at work in you, both to will and to work for His good pleasure. Do all things without grumbling or disputing; that you may prove yourselves to be blameless and innocent, children of God above reproach in the midst of a crooked and perverse generation, among whom you appear as lights in the world. (Phil 2:12-15 NASB)

Paul urges his readers to do all things without grumbling or disputing. To grumble means to murmur, to speak in a low tone of voice, to complain. The Greek word translated in the New American Standard Bible as "disputing" (elsewhere "arguing") connotes reasoning, questioning, and disputing. The Greek is *dialogismos* from close to the English "dialogue." The notion here is of disputing or questioning through the use of reasoning or dialogue—a back-and-forth discussion. Its use may be positive, neutral, or negative, depending on the context. Paul seems to use it in the negative sense.

Whining is just another term for this grumbling and disputing that Paul speaks of.

The New Testament concern with grumbling is based on the Old Testament. "And do not grumble, as some of them [Israelites in the wilderness] did—and were killed by the destroying angel" (1 Cor 10:10).

The Books of Exodus and Numbers are filled with references to the murmuring, grumbling, complaining—the whining—of the Israelites. They come to the Red Sea with Pharaoh close on their heels, and the complaints come pouring out. They run out of food in the desert, and suddenly Egypt seems like paradise by the wonder of selective memory. They forget about all the sorrows of Egypt and are obsessed instead with fantastic visions of life at the Cairo Hilton. God provides bread from heaven for them every day, but they get tired of the bread. And they begin to grouse like college sophomores complaining about the dormitory food, forgetting that they are a people on pilgrimage, a people on the march. When they run out of water, they forget how God has so wondrously provided for them, and the whining returns.

The more they complain, the more they grumble, the more they lose perspective on God's purpose for them and, eventually, the more they come under the hand of judgment. God makes it very clear to his people that they cannot complain their way into the promised land.

The people of Israel exemplify the condition of all mankind. In a sense they represent the whole human race and reflect the condition of the human heart. By nature we are not thankful and obedient. We are ungrateful and disobedient. There's no reason to be shocked and surprised when our children begin to whine. Like us, they come from a race of whiners.

In the Philippians passage I've just cited, grumbling and disputing is mentioned in the context of obedience. The chapter begins with the example of Jesus who, in his humility, was "obedient to the point of death." Paul then draws the lesson out for his readers: "So then, just as you have always obeyed . . . do everything without grumbling and disputing." To be like Jesus means to be obedient, and obedience is not the grumbling and whining obedience of dispute and complaint. It is willing, cheerful obedience.

Disobedience is one of the roots of whining behavior in children, just as it is in adults. Whining can be a way of deflecting, avoiding, disobeying a direction, without openly defying the authority. In order to train children to be obedient and respectful, it isn't enough simply to outlaw outright defiance:

DAD: Pick up your toys please.

JUNIOR: No! Pick 'em up yourself!

In order to train children to be obedient and respectful, we must also train them not to whine:

DAD: Pick up your toys please.

JUNIOR: Aw, Dad, do I have to?

"Do all things without grumbling and disputing."

Why Is This So Challenging?

Without a doubt, whining is one of the most challenging behaviors to deal with in raising small children. Three things about whining make it so troublesome.

First of all, whining is sneaky. Children don't suddenly begin whining in a way that grabs our attention. The four-year-old doesn't say, "Mom, I'd rather not do that. I'd like to whine instead." There are no "whine alarms" that sound once whining begins. Children develop the capacity to whine gradually as their verbal and cognitive skills develop. This process can be sneaky because it is so gradual. Parents are like the proverbial cold-blooded frog who hops into the pan of water at room temperature. The pan has just been placed on the electric stove, and the water heats up so gradually that the frog adjusts right along with it. Until his own blood boils.

Second, whining is slippery as well as sneaky. Open defiance, now that's something you can take hold of! But whining isn't like that. It's slippery and difficult to grab. It's measured in more subjective terms than outright disobedience—things like tone of voice and facial expression are often the key measures. In addition to the fact that it is often a matter of fine degrees, any one instance of whining doesn't seem "so bad" in itself.

Third, whining is infectious. Many cold victims are most infectious when the cold virus is in it's "sub-clinical phase" before the classic cold symptoms have arrived. How easy it is to be drawn by the sub-clinical cases of whining (the borderline cases of whining that we can barely recognize when alert, let alone when we are distracted) into our own form of whining. For example, you are on the phone with a friend, engaged in a pleasant conversation. Enter Molly, age four years. "Mo-om!" (the whining is there, but in seed form). You cover the mouthpiece with your hand and reply in the same tone of voice, "Molly! I'm on the phone."

Molly's whiner is getting wound up and she replies in that classic nasal tone of complaint as she moves from uneasiness and discontent to peevishness, "Mo-om, but I'm bored!"

Trying to keep the conversation with your friend going smoothly, you cup the mouthpiece again and match Molly with your own complaining tone of voice as you, too, move from uneasiness and discontent to peevishness, "Molly, will you please be quiet? Can't you see I'm on the phone?" Well, it's all downhill from there as you and Molly slide together down whining's slippery slope.

To say that whining is infectious and then cite a case where a mom "catches it" from her child isn't entirely fair to the children of the world. Because, as we all know, kids can catch colds from their moms and dads, too. One of the most challenging things about whining in our children is the fact that we whine as well. Not just in response to our kids' whining, but all by ourselves—without any prompting from Junior.

Now we've run into one of the truly imposing obstacles to raising our children in the "discipline and instruction of the Lord": ourselves.

Are we whining at the dinner table about the problems at the office or the troubles we face at home? Are we using those nasal complaining tones of voice, as we move from uneasiness and discontent to peevishness? Are we sniveling and complaining about the circumstances of our lives in a self-pitying way? Are we aiming to gain sympathy from others by the way we talk about our lives? We must face the fact that we are powerless to change our own whining ways. We must in humility give up on our own self-generated efforts and turn to Christ who alone has the power to set us free from this "body of sin and death." Lord, do in us what we cannot do in ourselves—make us like your own Son, who was obedient to the point of death, who like a lamb led to the slaughter did not raise his voice in complaint.

How Can We Help Our Children?

First of all, it helps if we can understand the three main sources of whining behavior.

1. Whining can be fueled by "atmospheric pressure." As mentioned above, whining is infectious. You can catch it. Children's whining behavior can be fueled by forces affecting the atmosphere of their environment. If whining is part of the home atmosphere, it will encourage your children to whine.

If you are still "under construction" in this area, don't let that prevent you from teaching, instructing, and training your child not to whine. We cannot wait until we are perfect before training our children in the way they should go. For example, I tend to be a little sloppy around the house. I used to be worse, but I'd rather be better as an example for my children. The fact that I tend to be sloppy doesn't help when it comes to training my kids to be tidy, but I can't exempt myself from my responsibility to train them. Sloppy or not, they only have one dad—and I'm it. I take concern to improve my own example, but I also have to insist that they keep their rooms straightened up.

Whining behavior can be fueled by other factors in the environment. Siblings and playmates may encourage whining. If they do, we may need to reduce the amount of time they spend together or supervise their time more closely. Over-exposure to television can also fuel whining behavior. The rampant materialism depicted on the television can encourage children not to be satisfied with what they have. The content of the programs they watch, often heavy with whining behavior, can affect them. I've also noticed that even with the finest programs, television induces a state of passivity in children (the glazed eyes, slack jaws, drooping brow) that makes them vulnerable to whining behavior. In order to deal with whining behavior effectively, it helps to take the "atmospheric pressures" into account and address them as we are able.

2. Whining can be fueled by underlying tension, fear, insecurity, and unresolved anger. Miriam was three years old and turning into a negative and grumpy child. Whining was natural to her negative disposition. When Miriam's dad told me about the situation, it was clear that Miriam was being disciplined appropriately, but something in the relationship with her parents was suffering. Her personality was getting under their skin and it was showing in the distance between them.

I suggested they put some extra effort into showing Miriam physical affection throughout the day. Her parents took the advice with great zeal and launched an affection campaign. They didn't stop the discipline; they merely added the affection. Miriam's mom reported that after a few days, she noticed a difference in Miriam's behavior. After a month, Miriam's personality had changed significantly. A friend of the family who hadn't seen Miriam for a while used to think of her as a sour puss. When the friend came over for a visit, she said, "What happened to Miriam? She's turning into such a delightful, positive, outgoing child." When Miriam's relationship with her mom and dad began to grow cool (largely as a result of Miriam's negative behavior), Miriam began to adopt a more negative feeling about life in general. The affection helped break the cycle and gave an added motivation to reduce the whining behavior.

Innumerable factors can make children more prone to whining—significant disruptions in the usual pattern of life, a death in the family, starting school, tensions and problems in school, increased tension between mom and dad or other members of the family. When insecurity is contributing to whining, often there will be other indications that a child is dealing with a higher than usual level of insecurity: regression in toilet training, waking up with bad dreams, more difficulty with separation anxiety, myriad little fears surfacing, from fears of getting flushed down the toilet to fear of the dark.

Part of the strategy for dealing with whining involves handling these issues. Many modern parents feel that if whining is fueled by anything like insecurity, then it is not helpful to provide the usual limits and discipline for whining. Certainly the source of insecurity should not be ignored and any efforts to help the child adjust will be helpful. And there may even be times when it is appropriate to relax the standards for whining behavior for a particular reason. But normally, it is most helpful to deal with the whining from both fronts: addressing the insecurity as well as providing the training—including correction, encouragement, and discipline—for whining. Part of training children to be obedient and respectful includes training them to observe certain behavioral norms even when their emotions are pressing them in another direction. Otherwise, children can simply come under the tyranny of responding to their emotions like a cork on the open seas.

3. Good old-fashioned willfulness. Even when other factors are contributing to whining behavior, this most common cause of whining is nearly always involved in whining behavior—the natural tendency for human beings to prefer their own way. It comes down to good old-fashioned willfulness, run-of-the-mill disobedience, garden-variety disrespect, the ever-present tendency toward folly.

In order to deal effectively with whining, we must apply the lessons of training in obedience to whining behavior.

Winning the War on Whining: A Training Approach

Three aspects of the training process are worth special attention when we are applying the lessons of training to the issue of whining: teaching, effective correction, and insisting.

Teach 'em about whining. The first step in training your child out of the whining habit is learning to identify what your child's whining behavior is in concrete, specific terms. Learn to recognize it yourself. Talk it over with your spouse. Break the whining behaviors down into concrete component parts— those facial expressions, the rolling of the eyes, the look of utter disgust are part of the whining syndrome; those inarticulate sounds, the groans and sighs too deep, as it were, for words are part of the whining syndrome; the tone of voice, that low, usually nasal tone of voice or that high-pitched sound may be part of the whining syndrome. Getting clear in your own mind about how your child whines will take some thoughtful observation, perhaps some discussion with a friend, and then some simple analysis.

If you are having a difficult time identifying your child's whining behavior, you may have a child who doesn't whine. Congratulations! Then again, you may simply be impervious. Ask someone who knows your child to help you identify his or her whining behaviors.

Once you are clear about how your child whines (and of one mind with your spouse about it) instruct the child in what whining is and how he does it. Be specific and concrete with your child: when you make these faces (demonstrate in graphic terms) you are whining. When you use this tone of voice (again, a demonstration please) you are whining. Those sighs and groans when I tell you to do something you don't want to do are whining. At first this process may seem like trying to grab hold of a pig coated in Crisco oil—but stick with it. Those greased pig contests are eventually won. To the persistent go the spoils. As your child learns that certain expressions are considered whining, he will no doubt try out others. Be more persistent than he is and continue to instruct.

Especially with young children, it is helpful to refer to all the behaviors associated with the whining syndrome with a single term (e.g., whining). In other words make it clear that all the various manifestations amount to one thing: whining.

Teach the child that whining is not acceptable. Teach him that grumbling isn't good for God's people. Teach him that it is a form of disobedience and disrespect—again, not good for us since God has told us to honor our parents so that it may go well with us. Don't just wait until you need to correct a child for whining to do the teaching. Teach him about whining when he *isn't* whining, at a time when he is most receptive.

Some kids have fairly predictable whining times such as before or after a nap or just before dinner. A word of instruction just before he or she moves into prime whining time can help.

Give effective correction when whining occurs. Most of us parents of whining children will feel that we do nothing but correct our children for whining. We despair of correction's value and grope for other answers to the whining problem. But I have been amazed to observe how infrequently many parents actually give clear, effective correction to their children for whining. It is not effective to correct a child sporadically for whining. Correction needs to take place whenever whining occurs. If you correct your child 15 percent of the time he whines, he will likely assume that 85 percent of his whining is acceptable—and with odds like that why bother to stop whining?

So to be effective, correction must be as persistent as the whiner's whining. Correction must also be clear and assertive.

The following table gives examples of typically nonassertive correction and the response we might imagine these corrections would evoke from the child.

Non-assertive Correction	*Child's Response*
"Why don't you stop whining like that?"	The child can think of several reasons.
"Your whining is driving me crazy!"	Child tempted to interpret this as success.
"How many times do I have to tell you to stop that?"	If you don't know, the child probably doesn't.
[In a whining tone of voice,] "Jimmy, *when* are you going to stop whining?"	Child remembers Jesus' words, "A student is not above his teacher."
"*Please* try to stop whining, won't you?"	Child knows you are about to give up.

The examples of clear and assertive correction are not nearly as imaginative, but they are more effective. My favorites include:

"Stop whining" and "Don't use that tone of voice with me. That's whining. Now stop it."

Making it stick. Children can know what whining is and receive a good dose of persistent, assertive correction. But to make it stick, a parent must be willing to insist that the whining stop and then must provide the necessary discipline if it doesn't. Otherwise, the war on whining won't be won.

First of all, make sure that whining does not become an effective way for the child to get his or her way. See that it doesn't work.

CHILD: [in classic nasal tone] Mo-om, (the whiner's name for mom) Jenny got a popsicle from Mrs. Vanderplough— can't I have one too?

MOM: Not when you ask like that.

Second, tell the child, in specific and concrete terms, how you want him to respond in place of the whining response. Then insist that he give the appropriate response.

MOM: Time for bed now, Julie.

JULIE: Bed! Already? Aw, Mom, I don't wanna go to bed!

MOM: Stop whining. I said it's time for bed now. Let me here a "Yes, Mom" in a decent voice.

Third, provide discipline as needed to make it clear that you are serious. Often more than an assertive word of correction is necessary.

DAD: Tom, come here, please.

TOM: Aw, Dad, come on . . . I just got started with my Lego blocks.

DAD: You heard me, Tom. Come here and stop that whining.

TOM: But I just sat down!

DAD: You're not obeying me: You will have to be punished for that.

Spanking as a form of punishment is especially suited for whining as a response to a parent's direction. Other forms of discipline (for example, sending a child to sit down in a "time out" chair for ten minutes) may also be used as long as the discipline is fairly immediate. (Telling a young child that he will have to go to bed fifteen minutes early for whining that occurs in the afternoon won't work.)

What If a Child Has a Firmly Established Whining Habit?

Those who have studied habit formation indicate that it often takes about six weeks to establish a habit. Presumably, it takes at least that long to replace one pattern of behavior with another. Many have tried to help their children with whining by engaging in a training process, only to give up after a few days or a week of effort. It is common for parents to try a number of different methods, but to stick to none. We try a little spanking, a little distraction, a little negotiation, and a little "tell him how his misbehavior makes you feel."

Most kids with an established pattern of whining can be helped by a thoughtful, consistent training process sustained over a period of weeks. Perhaps you now realize why this chapter is about winning the *war* on whining rather than winning the battle over whining. Launch your campaign during a week when you can find the energy to focus on this issue. Begin with a few days for teaching and help your child to identify whining behavior. During this time, teach, teach, teach. Don't worry so much about correction and punishment. Tell the child that on a certain day, you will begin to spank him if he does not respond to your correction about whining.

To begin the full-fledged training, including punishment, select the right day—a day when you are at your best, when you can make training your top priority, when you have a little more support around the house than usual. When "the Day" arrives, remind your child about whining and what it will result in today if he doesn't respond to correction. As a period of time goes by without any whining, encourage him: "Do you realize you haven't done any whining since breakfast? That's great. Well done!" When whining does occur, correct, and provide discipline as needed and promised. You shouldn't be of a mind to avoid the issue today. You should be alert to those occasions when you can engage your child in the training process. This, after all, is "the Day."

Take great pains to be consistent and alert for training opportunities for a few days in a row. During this time remember to pay special attention to showing favor and affection since the child will probably be receiving more than his normal share of discipline.

For the next six weeks, keep training your child in the whining area. Don't lose sight of the task. Talk it over regularly with your spouse. Tell a trusted friend what you are up to and give regular reports, if only to keep your attention focused.

Some kids are extraordinarily stubborn whiners. They may need the help of a reward system to supplement your training.

I know of a four-year-old who had a chronic problem with whining that did not respond to the normal training measures. We devised a reward system to help him break the whining habit. It worked. This boy wanted a baseball glove about as badly as a four-year-old can want anything. So the parents bought a large jar and a few large bags of marbles. They sat down with their son, placed the empty jar and the marbles in front of him, and pulled out a picture of a baseball glove. They told him that for the next few weeks at regular intervals they would have a "whine check." If, during that period of time, he was free of whining, he could place a marble in the jar. If he did any whining during that time, no marble for that time period. As soon as the jar was full of marbles, Dad would take him to the store to pick out one of those baseball gloves. They taped a picture of the baseball glove to the jar.

For the first few hours, they did a whine check every fifteen minutes to make sure he could get a taste of success. Then they held the checks every thirty minutes, and eventually to a more manageable hourly rate.

The reward system helped the child break the whining habit; and after a few weeks, with the jar full and the baseball glove in hand, they were able to return to the normal training process.

Putting It into Practice: Winning the War on Whining

1. Consider the specific whining behaviors you observe in your children. Consider things like:

• tone of voice
• posturing
• facial expressions

List the three most common whining behaviors you observe.

(1)——————————————————————————————

(2)——————————————————————————————

(3)——————————————————————————————

2. To help with the process of identification, keep track of your child's whining in a "Daily Whining Log." If his or her whining is less than continuous, simply note day, time, occasion for whining, specific expressions of whining, and probable cause of whining. If the whining is too frequent to note on each occasion, simply make a morning, afternoon, and evening entry. Note as best you can the specifics of the whining behavior. Do this for a few days. Then write your evaluation below.

——————————————————————————————

——————————————————————————————

——————————————————————————————

——————————————————————————————

——————————————————————————————

3. Sit down with your spouse or a trusted friend and discuss a plan to respond to the child's whining. Consider how you plan to teach, correct, and insist in the training process. Write it out.

- _____

- _____

- _____

- _____

- _____

- _____

- _____

- _____

4. In light of the most obvious whining problems you can identify in your children, identify what you consider the key steps to take in addressing the whining behavior:

- _____

- _____

- _____

- _____

> **Don't be discouraged! Remember that whining is the most challenging obedience issue to deal with.**

For Group Discussion and Support

1. Continue the encouragement campaign described in #1 of last chapter's "For Group Discussion and Support" for another third of the group's members.

2. Discuss the behaviors that constitute whining. Share some of the classic whining behaviors that you've observed in your own children.

3. Share what steps you think you could take to address your child's whining most effectively. Of these, which is the most personally challenging to you and why?

4. Close with prayer for one another. Pray for a spirit of thanksgiving, appreciation, and patience for the families in your group. Ask God to give you grace and strength to combat whining. End your time of prayer by interceding for the specific requests of group members. Thank God for the progress different group members have made thus far.

EIGHT

Training Young Children to Worship

IN THE LATE 1960s AND THROUGH THE 1970s, thousands of young people were touched by an outpouring of God's Spirit. Young men and women from pagan and nominally Christian backgrounds responded to a clear call to discipleship. At the time of the writing of this book, many of those affected by this work of God are still following the Lord, and many are active in local congregations, prayer groups, fellowships, and communities. And many are now parents of young children.

I've noticed something disturbing about the children of these parents who are themselves committed to Christ. In many congregations and prayer groups where these parents are gathered for worship, the children are either absent or present but not fully participating in the worship. The contrast is most striking in gatherings marked by expressive forms of worship—vigorous singing, hand clapping, raising of hands, and vocal acclamations of praise. In many of these settings, the children sit around gazing at the ceiling or reading books. Some are sprawled on the floor with a bag full of crayons, dolls, and toys. These children are not learning to worship God.

One could cite several reasons for this. Many children of

believing parents are highly influenced by their peers and by the world culture whose distinctive mark is intolerance and embarrassment at the thought of honoring God. They are living under the roof of a believing home, but the world is aggressively reaching out to them through television, friends, and school. One aspect of this challenge, the pervasive kiddie culture, will be addressed in the following chapter.

But there is another reason which accounts for the phenomenon: many parents do not value the necessity and importance, even the validity, of training their children to honor God, especially to honor God in worship. And those parents that do, don't know how to teach it. If you are one of those parents, uncertain of your responsibility to train your child to honor God or unsure of how to do it, this chapter is especially for you.

We begin by remembering that God created us to love and honor him and that he also insists on it.

> "I am the Lord your God. . . . You shall not make for yourself an idol. . . . You shall not bow down to them or worship them; for I, the Lord your God, am a jealous God. . . . You shall not misuse the name of the Lord your God, for the Lord will not hold anyone guiltless who misuses his name." (Ex 20:1, 4-5, 7)

God has a great jealousy or zeal for the honor of his name. God the Father is zealous for his Son's name. Jesus took Peter, James, and John with him to a high mountain. There he was transfigured before them—his body no longer wrapped in the mantle of humility, but for a time, charged with the glory of heaven. Moses and Elijah appeared with Jesus, and Peter mumbled something about preparing booths for all three. Just then, the cloud of the presence of God overshadowed them all, and a voice from the cloud said, "This is my Son, whom I have chosen; listen to him" (Lk 9:35). When the voice was gone, there was Jesus, as the account records, "by himself, alone."

The Father is filled with zeal for the honor of his Son's name, jealous that the glory belonging to his son not be in the least deflected.

In turn, the Son is zealous for his Father's name:

> When it was almost time for the Jewish Passover, Jesus went up to Jerusalem. In the temple courts he found men selling cattle, sheep and doves, and others sitting at tables exchanging money. So he made a whip of cords, and drove them from the temple area, both sheep and cattle; he scattered the coins of the money changers and overturned their tables. To those who sold doves he said, "Get these out of here! How dare you turn my Father's house into a market!" His disciples remembered that it is written: "Zeal for your house will consume me." (Jn 2:13-17)

We live in a generation which cares nothing for the honor of God's name—God's name is used like a sentence filler. But the life we now live, we live by faith in the Son of God. His life is in us and his consuming zeal for God's honor is in us as well.

We need to let the life of Christ rule the way we raise our children. That means taking very seriously our responsibility to train our children to love and honor God.

> Train a child in the way he should go, / and when he is old he will not turn from it. (Prv 22:6)

> Fathers ... bring them [your children] up in the training and instruction of the Lord. (Eph 6:4)

How ironic that so many believing parents are uncertain of their responsibility to train their children to honor and worship God. We are convinced of our responsibility to train them in personal hygiene, to train them for the future through educating them, but we are strangely squeamish about training them to honor and worship God. As we consider how to train our children to honor and worship God, we'll try to address some of the concerns that parents of the present generation typically struggle with.

How Do We Train Our Children to Honor God?

The three elements of the training process that we have focused on throughout apply to this area as well: modeling, teaching, and insisting. All three elements are needed whether we are training children to keep their rooms straight, to obey our instructions, or to honor God.

The Use of God's Name

First of all, as soon as the child learns to speak, we guard his use of God's name. We protect him from the danger of misusing the name of the Lord our God. Training our children in the use of God's name begins with our example. Do we misuse his name in our homes? Do we use his name to express our frustration? Do we use the name of God as an expletive: "[insert name of God], it's hot out there!" Do we tolerate TV programs that misuse God's name?

Training our children in the use of God's name continues with our teaching, which includes correction. Much of the teaching for young children boils down to correcting improper uses of God's name. If a child slips into misuse of his name, take the opportunity to correct and instruct. We've tried to prune expressions which are either derived from a profane use of God's name or which sound close to a misuse of God's name. For example, the expression "Geez" is derived from a profane use of the Lord's name, as is "Gosh darn."

After teaching and correction for early slips, children should be punished for misuse of God's name, normally with spanking. This is where many of us would feel a bit ill at ease. Spank a child because he's misused the Lord's name? Wouldn't that cause him to have negative associations with God—

precisely what we want to avoid? In fact, failure to punish the misuse of God's name results in something more spiritually troubling, a lack of genuine fear of God's name. Children *should* have a healthy fear of misusing God's name. Just punishment will reinforce this healthy fear of God. Shielding children from the reality of what it means for a creature to relate to the Creator is no service to them at all.

While this book is about young children, it should be noted that older children can easily slip into misuse of God's name as they come into greater exposure of it through others. This needs close attention. As the children get older this fundamental lesson in relating to God should not be lost. Misuse of God's name should be treated as a serious offense which elicits punishment.

Use of God's Word

Second, we train our children to honor God by including God's Word in their daily lives.

Hear, O Israel: The Lord our God, the Lord is one. Love the Lord your God with all your heart and with all your soul and with all your strength. These commandments that I give you today are to be upon your hearts. Impress them on your children. Talk about them when you sit at home and when you walk along the road, when you lie down and when you get up. (Dt 6:4-7)

This passage provides the basis for a Jewish prayer called the *Shema* (Hebrew for "hear"). As a devout Jew it is likely that Jesus grew up praying this prayer three times each day. By the time Jesus reached the age of twelve, he was conversant in the Scriptures—able to ask intelligent questions and give answers in his famous meeting in the temple with the elders.

Certainly his penetrating insight into God's Word had something to do with his identity as the Son of God. But he was also fully human and no doubt learned God's Word as any child would learn God's Word—through regular exposure to the Scriptures in his family.

We show honor by frequently referring to someone's words and perspective as especially important.

It is good to have a daily opportunity for children to hear a brief reading from the Bible. In our family, we include this at our dinner time, just after giving thanks but before we begin to eat. This sends an important message to the children: God's Word is important in this house. There are other ways to include God's Word in the life of children: Bible stories, simple memorization of Bible texts, and songs using God's Word as lyrics.

We are sometimes reluctant to do this because we think children cannot understand God's Word, that it is "over their heads." It is true that we need to keep it simple. We should do what we can to help the child understand. We can pick out the most simple and accessible thought, for example. Even then, much of it will go over the child's head. Nevertheless it is important, even for young children—and all the more as the children mature—to see that God's Word is important to mom and dad, that they refer to it often, that they view it as something to be obeyed. Meanwhile, you often discover that the child is picking up more than you thought.

Training in Honor by Example

Third, we train our child to love and honor God by expressing our own love and respect for God in the child's presence. Some time ago I noticed something in myself that I suspect is common among many of us. I found myself talking about God a great deal: at church, in my service to others, in small group fellowship settings. But how much was I expressing the importance of God in my life at home, at the dinner table—when I was with my wife and children? Not much. Our children cannot read our minds. We need to expose them to the love in our hearts, our esteem for God, the simple lessons we are learning from God and about God.

Let's remember to make simple expressions of our love for God, our gratitude to him, in the presence of our children. At the dinner table, think about what you have to be thankful for that day and share these small points of gratitude with the children. Report on answered prayers, small and great. One day my wife and I were trying to decide how to get our oldest daughter to a volleyball game she was playing in. We prayed for as long as it takes to say, "Lord, help us to find a ride for Maja." With ease, my wife found someone to pick her up and bring her back. That's not too small a matter to mention at dinner. Tell of an experience of God's presence or share a reflection prompted by a talk. Mention what you are reading in the Bible these days or an inspiring story in a book you're reading. Or tell a story you heard last week about God's mercy to someone. More times than not, there is *something* we can say to express the fact that God exists and has a personal concern for us and the people around us.

Don't expect this kind of simple communication to elicit an enthusiastic response. When I mentioned that the Lord helped us with the small request to find a ride for Maja to the volleyball game, the children didn't look up from their broccoli with an enraptured expression and say in unison, "Don't we have a wonderful God?" It was enough for them to see that God is involved in our lives, even in small matters, and to be exposed to the gratitude of mom or dad. The primary purpose in sharing these things with your children is not to "get a response" but to reveal to them in concrete terms what is in your heart and mind about God.

Training in the Simple Things

Finally we train children to love and honor God by modeling, teaching, and insisting on the simple things that human beings (including children) can do to show honor to

God. Of course, properly understood, "the things human beings do to show honor to God" could include the whole range of actions that are part of a righteous life: the thoughts and intentions of the heart, good deeds that glorify the Father, concern for the poor, love of the brethren, and many other things. But my focus here is on the simple physical expressions of honor. Most of them have to do with how we worship God or conduct ourselves at times set aside for worship. While it is a mistake to consider these simple expressions as constituting the whole of what one does to honor God, it is also a mistake to underestimate the value of these expressions, especially in training children in giving honor and glory to God.

Like verbal and physical expressions of love and relationship between those close to each other, ("I love you," physical affection, offering your seat to someone you wish to honor, and so on) expressions of worship and honor to God are a key to encouraging and disposing us toward other expressions of honor (obedience, faithfulness, good works). While not an end in themselves, God has given us explicit directions about how we are to express our honor toward him in simple acts of worship. Many parents didn't learn these things themselves until they were young adults. But, in fact, they are the kind of simple expressions that children are able to learn and do.

Honor Expression #1: Paying attention with your body (alias: "Sit/stand still"). Parents train their children to honor God by training them to "pay attention with their bodies" when attending family devotions, listening to the reading of God's Word, attending church, and other gatherings devoted to worship.

It is common to hear parents complain about how difficult it is for their young children to participate in public worship. But the answer to this problem is not simply to make the services more entertaining for the children or to send them off to be entertained elsewhere. Parents have a responsibility to train their children in how to participate in a worship setting. If we wait until children graduate from the nursery to begin attending portions of worship services (or the whole service) and hope that somehow they will be able to handle themselves, we won't be pleasantly surprised. Like everything else kids do, they need to learn how to participate in worship, and they need to learn at home.

By the time a child is twelve months old, mom can begin to train the child to sit still on her lap—first for very brief periods, then gradually lengthening the time. This training includes teaching the child what "sit still" means. Once again, training means teaching, correcting, praising, and insisting. Once the young child knows and refuses to hold still for a brief time, give him or her a light spanking in order to insist.

Family devotions provide a training ground for public worship—little training sessions with mom, followed by insisting that the child hold still for manageable periods of family prayer. Learning to hold reasonably still for five or ten minutes of family prayer around the dinner time or before bedtime is much more manageable for a young child than a ninety-minute worship service. Do the simple steps of training: teach, correct, praise small steps forward, and insist (including discipline if needed).

While there is an exception to most every rule, generally speaking most children can be trained by the age of two years to sit attentively (that is, sitting quietly, with a minimum of squirming and need for physical restraint and supervision) for about twenty minutes. Longer periods will be more challenging, but they are also possible.

Similarly, young children can be taught to stand reasonably still as an expression of honor during family prayer and public worship. The same kind of process, beginning with requiring brief times of standing still and then extending what is required as the child matures, is called for. Remember that standing is a biblical expression of respect. It is good to teach children that standing attentively is a way of showing honor to God.

> Rise in the presence of the aged, show respect for the elderly
> and revere your God. I am the Lord. (Lv 19:32)

> He said to me [Ezekiel, at the time when God commissioned
> him], "Son of man, stand up on your feet and I will speak to
> you." (Ez 2:1)

By the time a child is four or five years old, he should be able
to stand at a worship service when his parents are standing and
sit when they are sitting. During extended periods of standing
he may need to sit down for a few minutes, then resume
standing. Again, I offer this as an indication of what is
reasonable to expect when a child is trained. Without training,
most four or five year olds are not inclined to do this.

I've found that focusing on a few simple rules goes a long
way to helping them participate in worship:

1. Face forward at all times.
2. Feet off the seat in front of you.
3. Sit in the chair provided (no sprawling on the floor).
4. Do what mom and dad are doing (stand when they stand,
sit when they sit, kneel when they kneel, and so on).

I think it is a mistake to entertain the children by bringing a
bag full of toys for them to play with during worship. This only
sanctions the idea that the activity of worship is not for them. It
actually teaches them to tune out.

For some children, adaptations may be necessary for par-
ticularly long services or gatherings, such as an especially long
talk. Some kids may not be able to stand for long periods of
time without a brief time to sit or to be held. Some children will
need more supervision than others. But for the most part, these
are attainable with training and reasonable to require.

When faced with the challenge, we parents are likely to
wonder, "Is it really worth the trouble to train kids in these
matters?"

It is. Remember, there is a connection between learning to
sit and stand appropriately and showing respect toward God.

We're involved in something that goes beyond mere socialization for human company. Second, the alternatives to training are often simply tension between parents and restless children. Parents are reduced to glaring at their children to settle them down, yanking their arms, not to mention pleading, cajoling, and bribery—all very undignified. Third, the issue of learning self-control begins with children learning to control their bodies. Children who don't learn to control their bodies often are slow to grow in the wider issues of self-control. Young children who don't learn how to handle themselves in worship may well become scowling adolescents with folded arms, a mouth full of gum, and a body language that indicates their preference to be anywhere else.

Honor Expression #2: Singing to the Lord.

> Sing to the Lord a new song, / his praise in the assembly of the saints. (Ps 149:1)

> How good it is to sing praises to our God, / how pleasant and fitting to praise him! (Ps 147:1)

Singing is one of the chief means human beings have of expressing honor, love, adoration, and praise to God. The heavenly worship is filled with singing. Singing is one of those happy combinations of something enjoyable, fun, and commanded (as the psalmist says, it is "pleasant and fitting").

From the earliest age children should be encouraged to sing. Singing is part of the worship of God's people and should be happening in the home as well as in public assemblies. Even if you aren't the Von Trapp family, singing to the Lord honors God and can be part of your worship at home. As children are able to sing, they should be expected to sing. If you know that your child is able to sing, that he knows a particular song, you should be able to direct him to sing if for some reason he is "not in the mood." Refusal (not inability or not knowing a particular song) to sing should be treated as any other kind of refusal. As in all of these matters, the more singing kids do in the home, the more they will participate in singing in public worship.

Honor Expression #3: Hand clapping.

Clap your hands all you nations; / shout to God with cries of joy. / How awesome is the Lord Most High, / the great King over all the earth! (Ps 47:1)

The clapping of hands is an expression of acclamation—a way of recognizing God as the exalted king. Clapping is a simple gesture that children are quite capable of doing. It is an expression they can easily associate as giving honor since it is one of the few signs of approval or acclamation in our culture (applause). Clapping is most common as an accompaniment to singing, but there is no reason it cannot be done apart from song as an act of acclaiming the greatness of God.

This takes a little instruction and leadership. In family prayers, dad or mom says, "God is a great king; let's take some time to clap before him to acclaim him."

In leading family worship, train your children to do these things. Model, teach, and insist. Give simple directions expecting the children to respond as they would to any other direction. Don't allow your children to ignore your direction in these matters.

Honor Expression #4: Lifting hands in praise.

May my prayer be set before you like incense; / may the lifting up of my hands be like the evening sacrifice. (Ps 141:2)

I will praise you as long as I live, / and in your name I will lift up my hands. (Ps 63:4)

Hear my cry for mercy / as I call to you for help, / as I lift up my hands / toward your Most Holy Place. (Ps 28:2)

The lifting of hands is the biblical expression of praise as well as supplication (for the latter, remember Moses lifting his hands in intercession as the Israelites engaged in battle). Most children will not automatically lift hands in prayer, unless someone teaches them how to do it. This is not to say that young children, during the time when they are especially inclined toward imitation, will not spontaneously raise their hands in prayer. However, for many children in our culture, self-consciousness and natural inhibition will easily quench the practice if they do not learn that it is a fitting expression of worship. And, of course, children, like adults, will be deeply influenced by the practice of others in their environment. If in public worship it is not normal for the participants to lift hands in prayer, no amount of training in the practice will help them to do it. In other words, it is only likely that they can learn to do this where there is a supportive environment, whether in the family or in public worship.

Many would equate this particular expression of worship with the Pentecostal and charismatic movements, since the practice is only normative (beyond a pastor, priest, or other presiding leader) within settings influenced by those movements. In fact, the practice of lifting hands is not necessarily connected theologically to a particular understanding of the impartation or infilling of the Holy Spirit, any more than kneeling or standing attentively in God's presence or singing is.

I mention this for two reasons. If the reader is refraining from lifting hands in prayer on the grounds that his theology of the Holy Spirit is different than the theologies of those for whom the practice is more common, I would urge him to reconsider. It is an expression of worship enjoined by the Scriptures, just as kneeling and singing are enjoined in the Scriptures for those who would worship God. Why shouldn't you lift your hands in prayer and teach your children to do likewise?

If the reader is involved in worship where lifting of hands is normative, it is likely in a setting influenced by the Pentecostal or charismatic movements. I've noticed that many parents in these settings have the notion that it is not proper to teach their children to lift their hands in worship until such time as they receive an impartation of the Spirit as older children or adults. They feel that to do so would be like expecting their children to speak in tongues or exercise other gifts of the Spirit before being baptized in the Spirit (or whatever term might be used). This is often because in their own experience, these parents did not even think to lift their hands in prayer until they experienced an impartation of the Spirit or began at least to be open to exercising spiritual gifts, such as speaking in tongues.

To these parents I would say the same thing: why not teach your young children to lift their hands in prayer? Why wait until they have experienced an impartation of the Spirit that corresponds to your experience as an adult? The lifting of hands in prayer is enjoined in the Scriptures. It was a normative biblical expression of worship even before the Pentecostal outpouring of the Spirit promised under the New Covenant! If you teach your child to pray to God as Father, or to kneel as a sign of reverence, why not also teach him to lift his hands in prayer? Children are by nature masters of the concrete. The distinction between their minds and their bodies is even less clear to them than it is to us. We don't help them to worship God at their young age by neglecting to train them to do the concrete expressions of worship using the bodies God has given us.

Let me share a bit about how this has worked in our own family. I never took the opportunity with our older two children to train them in certain ways of worshiping God, including the lifting of the hands. The training I gave them on how to conduct themselves in worship included teaching them to sit and stand respectfully and attentively within reason. We also taught them to pray simple prayers at dinner and bedtime.

At the age of thirteen, my oldest daughter attended a camp for girls her age, sponsored by our community, The Word of

God. In that setting the girls were encouraged to be more expressive in worship, and by the end of the camp, things like lifting hands, singing aloud together, and speaking out their praises to God became normative. After camp, Maja and I had a talk about her newfound freedom in worship. She said that she genuinely wanted to continue to walk in her new freedom. But she explained her concern that her natural inhibition and the fact that she wasn't used to doing things like lifting her hands in family prayers might make it difficult.

At that point, I told her that I thought it had been a mistake for me not to teach her earlier how to worship God through the simple expressions of worship found in the Bible. She agreed that if she had learned to do these things as a younger child, she would be less self-conscious and inhibited. I told my daughter that from then on, I would not neglect my responsibility to train her in some of the practical ways of doing what was her life's highest priority—offering praise and worship to God. I let her know that I would teach her how to worship according to the biblical norms, and that, like other important things in her life, I would insist on it, to help her overcome her inhibitions.

Maja needed some additional teaching about lifting her hands. "No, don't lift up your arms with your hands hanging limp from the wrist, do it this way." She needed some correction. If I said, "Let's lift our hands in worship now," and Maja responded lethargically or not at all, I spoke to her about it. Maja knew that if she didn't respond to teaching and correction as she was able, she would be punished. This wasn't necessary because she was already accustomed to obedience. But I'm sure the fact that it was a possibility helped her to respond.

Some time later I asked her a question about this topic. "Maja, when you were younger, I occasionally used to encourage you kids to lift your hands to praise God, but I never insisted on it. Do you remember that? And what did you think about that?" She replied, "I guess I figured you weren't that serious about it since you didn't insist on it. I figured it must not be that important."

Sometimes we hesitate to train our children to worship because our children indicate that they don't feel like expressing their worship. Sometimes they say they don't want to. But often, in fact, they simply don't feel like it. Remember how liberating it was to realize that worship doesn't depend on our feelings? That we don't have to wait until we are overwhelmed with a "worship mood," that we can decide to worship God because he's worthy and we know it's right and good to do? Our children desperately need to learn this lesson so that they are no longer in bondage to the fickleness of their feelings! They learn this lesson as we train them to worship God: as we model, teach, and insist.

"But," we respond, "should we insist that they do simple acts of worship to God if they don't want to, if they are not choosing to?"

Here we must remember that we are commanded to worship God. Do you allow a child who is under your authority to blaspheme God? Of course not! We are commanded not to blaspheme. Do we ask a child under our authority whether he wants to come with us to church, or once there, whether he wants to hang out in the lobby or join us for the worship service? A time will come when our children will not be under our authority in the same way that they are now. A time will come when they must choose for themselves whether to serve Christ or not. Until that time, we train them to do what is right. We work with them to do what is right with a good attitude. "Train a child in the way he should go, and when he is older, he will walk in it," the Book of Proverbs tells us.

Honor Expression #5: Verbally expressed praise. The biblical directions about worship emphasize verbal, expressive, and vigorous praise.

Clap your hands all you nations; / shout to God with cries

of joy. / ... God has ascended amid shouts of joy, / the Lord amid the sounding of trumpets. / Sing praises to God, sing praises; / sing praises to our King, sing praises. (Ps 47:1, 5-6)

Come, let us sing for joy to the Lord; let us shout aloud to the Rock of our salvation. (Ps 95:1)

May the praise of God be in their mouths [not merely in their minds]. ... (Ps 149:6)

From the lips of children and infants / you have ordained praise. (Ps 8:2)

This is what the Lord says: "Sing with joy ... / shout for the greatest of the nations. / Make your praises heard. ..." (Jer 31:7)

From a very young age, children can learn to speak aloud simple prayers of praise and thanksgiving to God. The prayers of the Bible include very simple refrains that young children are able to use, (e.g., "Praise the Lord," "The Lord is good," "The Lord is King"). Prayers of simple thanksgiving and the prayers of acclamation (prayers ascribing God's qualities or using his various titles) are especially suited for young children.

Like adults, children need to learn how to pray. As Dietrich Bonhoeffer—a Lutheran theologian who was a leader in the confessing church in Germany resisting the Nazi regime—has said, biblical prayer is not simply "pouring out whatever is in our hearts to God." Biblical prayer is prayer in and through Jesus. We don't pray in our own name, we pray in his name. We don't know how or what to pray apart from him, but he teaches us to pray. Children are no better off than adults. They, too, need to be taught how to pray.

The above list of expressions of worship is not meant to be exhaustive. The principles apply to the other biblical expressions or postures of worship, such as bowing and kneeling.

The Setting for Training in Worship

The need to train our children in worship points to the importance of a daily time when the family can worship God together. The particular format and time for daily family prayers can vary a great deal, depending on the needs and circumstances of a given family, as well as any church traditions of family prayer.

Our family has family prayers before dinner. We gather around the table before dinner and stand at our seats. My son passes out copies of the New Testament and Psalms (all in the same version), one to each person. We begin by praying a psalm together, using a rotation of psalms posted on the china cabinet. Depending on the psalm, we either pray the psalm in unison or have all those who can read, read an individual verse in sequence. This is followed by a time of vocal praise where everyone speaks aloud simple prayers of praise and acclamation together. This period of a few minutes at times includes lifting of hands, a short song, and clapping. I then either pray or assign someone to say a prayer of thanks for the meal.

After family prayer, we sit down and I read a selection from the Bible, again using a pattern of readings. During special seasons of the year, such as Advent or the forty days before Easter, we may include some prayers focusing on the theme of the season. For example, during Advent we light a candle on the Advent wreath, accompanied by some responses focusing on the Lord's coming. After dinner, we sometimes take a few minutes to work on memorizing a psalm together which we can include in our family prayers so that the children who don't read can participate.

We also take time every Saturday night to celebrate the beginning of the Lord's Day (according to the Hebrew reckoning of days: sunset to sunset). The celebration includes blessing a cup of wine or grape juice, sharing a loaf of bread, and lighting a candle, followed by a meal. It includes responses that the young children soon memorize as we do it each week.

(See *Celebrating the Lord's Day,* a booklet published by Servant Books, 1986.) This provides us with a more structured opportunity for family worship. The particular format or the seasonal variations are not nearly as important as having time each day for family prayer.

Conclusion

The Son of God is living among his people. He is present by his Spirit in our families. And he is zealous for the honor of God's name. He is alive in us to bring honor to God through us, through our families, through our children. As we train our children to honor God, we will ourselves be renewed in our zeal, as the zeal of the Son of God for his Father's house rises up within us. And over time, our homes will become a place where Christ is honored, where our children and others can grow in the highest call extended to human beings—the call to worship the holy King.

Putting It into Practice: Training Young Children to Worship

1. Review with your spouse the area of misusing the Lord's name. Examine whether you use or allow any profane uses of God's name. Take a couple of weeks to purge these expressions from your own vocabulary, then begin to train your children in the proper use of God's name.

2. Plan a format for daily family prayer to use in your family. For example:

- Sing a short chorus
- Pray a psalm aloud together
- A short period for simple prayers of praise, thanksgiving, and acclamation spoken aloud together
- Pray for a few specific needs
- Pray "the Lord's Prayer"

List the elements you would like to include in order:

- _____

- _____

- _____

- _____

- _____

3. List the physical expressions of worship that your children already do.

- _____

- _____

- _____

- _____

4. Consider what other physical expressions of worship you would like to teach your children. List two of them below:

(1)_____

(2)_____

Select one and begin the training process.

For Group Discussion and Support

1. Discuss the concept of training children to worship. In what ways is the idea new to you? What aspect do you find most challenging?

2. Share anything you are currently doing as a family to help your children to worship. Mention one or two specific steps that you think you ought to take.

3. End with a time of prayer. Ask God to help your children worship him in spirit and in truth.

NINE

The Influence of Kiddie Culture

A CHRISTIAN LEADER FROM A TRIBAL VILLAGE in Africa was visiting a friend of mine. The guest was the father of several children. His village was, by Western standards, primitive. It consisted of thatched-roof huts and had no running water, no electricity, and no medical care. His life was not what an American would call attractive. In addition to the hardships of normal life, Christians in that region were persecuted. In fact, this man returned to his village to find that it had been ransacked. A number of Christian leaders had been murdered. Had he been there, he surely would have been killed.

But this father was not impressed by American culture. He said to my friend, "I'm so glad I live where I do. I would hate to raise my children in this country. There are just too many things pulling them away from God."

To raise children for Christ requires a sober assessment of the environment in which we are living.

Do not love the world or anything in the world. If anyone loves the world, the love of the Father is not in him. For everything in the world—the cravings of sinful man, the lust of the eyes and the boasting of what he has and does—comes not from the Father but from the world. (1 Jn 2:15-16)

We are attempting to raise our children in the context of a wider environment that is shaped by influences antithetical to believing and obeying Jesus. It is a secular environment, fundamentally at odds with the kingdom of God.

The power of the "world," in this sense of the term, is based on its appeal to something in us which C.S. Lewis has described as being "bent": the "cravings of sinful man, the lust of the eyes, and the boasting of what he has or does." The world is a powerful agent for evil because it latches onto that thing that is "bent" in us and pulls us away from faith and obedience to Christ: "For our struggle is not against flesh and blood, but against the rulers, against the authorities, against the powers of this dark world and against the spiritual forces of evil in the heavenly realms" (Eph 6:12).

In fact, this appeal of the world's culture is part of a broader spiritual battle raging all around us—a spiritual struggle energized by demonic forces at odds with God, jealous of human beings called to represent God.

Let's take a look at how this affects our children and try to understand its manifestations in our secular culture. It will take some analysis of our own situation before we can evaluate how best to take action. So stay tuned.

Youth and Kiddie Culture

It doesn't take a prophet or a seer to understand how this seductive worldview works on teenagers in Western culture. Mike Keating, a leader of University Christian Outreach, wrote a series of articles for *Pastoral Renewal* magazine titled "Highway to Hell." The articles outline a phenomenon that Keating refers to as "youth culture."

Through culture carriers like powerful peer groups and a media blitz epitomized by the anti-Christian and, in many cases, anti-human values of popular rock music, teenagers in Western culture are being drawn into a way of life headed toward spiritual death. Indicators such as a high incidence of suicide and premarital sex among teenagers, including those who would identify themselves as Christians, suggest that youth culture is a powerful and dangerous influence.

The powers operative in youth culture, if judged by their fruits, are certainly of demonic origin. These powers are by no means satisfied to influence only teenagers. We see signs of the same strategy aimed at younger children, including pre-schoolers.

The strategy is simple: (1) Develop a distinct culture that takes hold among young children, quite separate from the adult world and shaped by influences rooted in the kingdom of this world. (2) Market this culture aggressively among children through television, advertising, toys, music tapes, books, and other attractive items for sale so that individual children and the peer environment are influenced. (3) Promote, in embryonic form, values and influences which will prepare children for more dangerous influences later on. That's when youth culture begins to get its foot inside the door of our children's world. (See "The Media and Youth Culture," Jacek Popiel; *Pastoral Renewal* June, 1987.)

The words of Jesus when he sent his disciples into a crooked generation to proclaim the gospel are words of instruction and warning for parents raising children in modern culture: "Be as shrewd as snakes and as innocent as doves" (Mt 10:16). Jesus was warning his disciples to be discerning, to be wise, to be shrewd about the environment into which he was sending them. What a need in our day, in our circumstances, for discernment! This is one of our chief duties as parents: to be discerning about the influences shaping our children. To be disciples who are "as shrewd as serpents and as innocent as doves," we need to understand that young children are, in fact, the targets of an aggressive marketing campaign rooted in the kingdom of this world. It's an aggressive campaign because it's driven by the power of money, a very powerful influence in our society. Consider, for example, how aggressively and effectively some of the fast-food franchises have marketed their products among children. Consider the corporate mascots, the attractive playgrounds adjoining the restaurants, the endless promotions aimed at children, and so on. What kid doesn't know Ronald McDonald by name in our culture?

The economic reasons for marketing aimed at children are obvious: (1) Kids have increasing influence in families. A network news report focused on the fact that advertising for certain adult products is increasingly aimed at children because of the growing influence children have in their families over what products are purchased. (2) Kids have more money to spend than ever before and more opportunities to spend it. As family size decreases and life expectancy rises, more folks are buying more presents for fewer children. (3) Many corporations have a long-range strategy with marketing aimed at securing the loyalty of future generations.

The fact is children are the targets of massive marketing campaigns, and the marketing campaigns are effective. And more than just hamburgers are being promoted in this way. Much of what's promoted among children is rooted in the ways of the world—the "cravings of sinful man, the lust of the eyes, and the boasting of what he has and does." In fact, there seems to be something developing among children that is similar to what's happening among our older youth. We see a culture not shaped by parents or interacting with the adult world, but a world of its own. It is largely shaped by the world, the flesh, and the devil. Its strategy is to isolate even young children from the way of life of their parents. We might call it "kiddie culture."

Rock Music

We need to be able to discern the specific influences of the world in the various expressions of kiddie culture. For example, kiddie culture is marked by a downward infiltration of rock music. Some rock groups are, from a marketing perspective, aimed at eleven and twelve-year-olds, but the downward infiltration is finding its way into the elementary and pre-school world. With increasing frequency, rock music personalities are promoted among very young children. When my son was in elementary school, Michael Jackson had quite a following among his peers. He was known, idolized, and imitated widely by elementary school-age children. A cartoon heroine at the time of the writing of this book is named "Jem"—a girl who is transformed into a rock 'n roll momma by magical power, who goes on to save the world and crush the enemy with her music. One of the "Defenders of the Universe," a popular line of high-tech toys, is equipped with an electric guitar that becomes a sonic blaster destroying evil through rock 'n roll. A major toy manufacturer offers "Dancin' Rocker Barbie" for ages four and up.

The problem with this downward infiltration of rock music is quite simply the effects of the music's underlying themes of rebellion toward authority, of sensuality, and of isolation from the adult world.

Low Value on Obedience and Respect for Parents

Much of the entertainment in the kiddie culture which influences children reinforces the modern distaste for authority. Frequently parents or other authority figures are portrayed unsympathetically. Popular children's book characters often portray fathers, in particular, as buffoons. It seems they're always making mistakes and doing stupid things. The children in these stories are often in the position of humoring an inept father. Several popular science fiction movies portray understanding children in touch with benign extra-terrestrials who must be protected against misinformed and bigoted authority figures like the police, their own parents, or governmental officials. This increases the sense of alienation between the adult world and the world of the child.

Rarely is disobedience to parents portrayed in a negative light. A recent car commercial features a teenage girl who calls her boyfriend with the good news that her parents have just left her alone in the house. Would he like to come over? The youth is ecstatic over his good fortune and drives through a rainstorm to the sounds of a popular song, "When a Man Loves a Woman." When he arrives to find the father unexpectedly home, the viewers' sympathy is with the disappointed young couple.

The Occult

But there is even more cause for alarm. Kiddie culture is increasingly marked by occult symbols and concepts. Movies from famous producers like Lucas and Speilberg are filled with non-Christian religious influences. For example, the popular "Star Wars" movies are based on an Eastern dualist worldview where the "Force" is both good and bad. This is a far cry from a holy God in whom there is no darkness at all. The movie "Raiders of the Lost Ark" treated the sacred Ark of the Covenant from the Old Testament—which is uniquely associated with the presence of the God of Abraham, Isaac, and Jacob—as an occult object of ambiguous spiritual origins. The movie "Gremlins" featured cute, seemingly benign spiritual creatures traditionally understood to be demonic. In an inversion typical of the occult, the gremlins took over a town on Christmas Eve.

Whether or not these movies are viewed by your children, the movies become the basis for cartoons, comics, toys, and video games. Many of the most popular and influential cartoon characters are transformed by supernatural powers which in one way or another are spiritual in origin. Figures like Superman, whose powers were not so clearly spiritual (Superman was simply a big fish in a little pond; a man of average strength on his home planet, but with supernatural strength on earth), have been superseded by figures who draw spiritual power from spiritual sources other than the God and Father of our Lord Jesus Christ.

Have you ever felt downright uncomfortable watching a five-year-old boy whip out his play sword, point it to the sky, and proclaim, "I have the power!"? He's been watching "Masters of the Universe." These receive power in various ways, some by the "power of Gray Skull." The female counterpart to the cartoon figure "He-man" is "She-Ra." "Ra" is the ancient sun god of Egypt. The ideological influence of radical feminism with its attraction to occult spirituality that centers around women and a positive view of witchcraft is evident in the kiddie-culture menu. Many cartoons feature "good witches" who are connected with sources of spiritual power. Radical feminist ideology would view this as a positive step toward breaking down the patriarchal influence characteristic of biblical religion.

Another Kiddie Culture
Characteristic: the "Pride of Life"

"For all that is in the world, the lust of the flesh and the lust of the eyes and the pride of life, is not of the Father but is of the world" (1 Jn 2:16 RSV). The New International Version translates "the pride of life" as "the boasting of what he [sinful man] has and does," which is a good description of our exaltation of technology as the ultimate solution to the problems of man.

A popular cartoon series at the time of the writing of this book is "The Masters of the Universe." The makers of this cartoon combine occult spirituality with this exaltation of human technology. One of the favorite Jewish titles for God is "Master of the Universe." What name for a group of cartoon figures could be more arrogant?

Many of the most popular toys and video games are rooted in this fascination with the power of technology. They foster an unhealthy focus on technology. They give the impression that the universe can be mastered by man through his technology—a concept which is rooted in the pride of life.

Premature and Worldly Sophistication

Kiddie culture also presents to young children all the trappings of adult and often worldly sophistication. Situation comedies present children "dressed to kill," boogeying like their older brothers and sisters. We see mere children eagerly engaging in the world of erotic attraction well before puberty has set in.

A commercial shows a father picking up his pre-pubescent daughter from a school dance, driving her to mix with the boys at the local fast-food joint. He begins to go into the restaurant with her, but his daughter's pleading look sends him back to the car to sit and wait and ponder poignantly the newness of love. A computer commercial features an eleven or twelve-year-old boy with all the looks and moves of a network news anchor man, dressed like a model from a slick, stylish catalogue. A guest on a radio talk show gives advice to parents of elementary schoolchildren who are hard pressed to keep up with the cost of decking out their kids in the latest designer fashion. Meanwhile, back in the local elementary school, the girls are mimicking the sultry look of the most recent media phenomenon.

Young children are undeniably under these kinds of pressures. All of this works its way into the children's peer environment and "leans on" them to get sophisticated fast. The children, in turn, pressure their parents. For fear of the unthinkable prospect of "making my child stand out," the parents then yield. Indeed, something powerful is at work to shape the lives of our children. And its influence is everywhere.

The Carriers of Kiddie Culture

Kiddie culture is transmitted through the combination of TV programs, movies, music groups, and toys. For example, when Michael Jackson was "hot" there were Michael Jackson cartoons, toys, movies, sweatshirts, fast-food restaurant promotions, plastic glasses with every fill-up at the gas station, comic books, comic strips in the newspapers, coloring place mats at family restaurants, Pepsi commercials, sequin gloves, and moon-walking contests in the playgrounds of the elementary schools. Here we see the need to appreciate how kiddie culture functions as a pervasive and powerful influence on our children.

Some of the most influential carriers of kiddie culture are daily cartoons shown before and after school. At the time of the writing of this book, they were: "Masters of the Universe"; "GI Joe"; "She-Ra"; "Jem"; "Transformers"; "Defenders of the Universe." *Business Week* magazine (March 25, 1985) reports on a disturbing development in the toy industry—the powerful marketing combination of cartoon figures advertised in commercials and featured in their own programs:

> Masters of the Universe is representative. Adam, Skeletor, and the others began their existence not as the brainchildren of cartoonists but as toys created by Mattel, Inc. Then, in a joint effort with Filmation Studios, the company developed a TV show based on the characters as part of a coordinated package to promote and sell the toys. . . . The number of toy-based shows has jumped from 14 to 40 in the past two years. Mattel's Masters of the Universe line—priced from $5 to $30—racked up $500 million in worldwide sales in 1984.

The characters of these programs will evolve until they wear out. Other characters will replace them. But the direction of the values being reinforced is not likely to change.

Meanwhile, their influence among children is impressive. The kids watch the cartoons, buy the toys, play with the toys based on the cartoons—re-enacting the scenes from the cartoons in a kind of spoon-fed imaginative play. The toy companies come out with more characters and paraphernalia. Children are able to form profound identifications with their favorite cartoon figures, reinforced by the cartoons, toys, lunchboxes, looseleaf notebooks, cassettes, comics, and books. We need to realize that we aren't dealing with isolated influences but something that can exercise a powerful and pervasive influence on our own children.

The problem with the influences of kiddie culture is not that they will automatically turn our young children into worshipers of technology, vain and worldly women, occult practitioners, or rock music junkies. The problem is that this is all contrary to what we are teaching our children about the kingdom of God. As these influences go unchallenged, the children are çaught in a confusing array of mixed messages. If the characteristics of kiddie culture are seen as "normal" and "harmless," then the groundwork has been laid which will make them susceptible to worse influences later on.

So What Do We Do about All This?

As disciples we are warned not to fall in love with the world. We are warned to be discerning, "as wise as serpents and as innocent as doves." As parents and adults with influence over children, we are the ones who have to do something about this if anything is to be done. So what do we do?

First of all, we should pay attention to kiddie culture and exercise spiritual discernment for our children. Sometimes discernment is a very straightforward process, based on clearcut criteria. But some things don't quite work that way. Sometimes you just have to "sniff it out." A Christian leader from another country once came to visit the Christian community that I am part of. He had read about our community life and been exposed to some of the publications originating from it. When he arrived he said, "We come to Ann Arbor to sniff you out and see what kind of dogs you are." No doubt in his original language, it had a more charming ring to it than that. But the point was clear: he came to exercise discernment about the kind of life we were living.

Much of kiddie culture is easy to discern by objective criteria. A toy called "Supernatural Ghost Warriors" with a macabre look and glowing yellow-green eyes is obviously not drawing from the right spiritual well. But some things are not so clearly discerned. We are left to "sniff it out," to get a feel for whether it is suitable or not.

Kids are great at pressing us for reasons, especially when we say "no." But there are times when you just don't think a particular television program or toy is appropriate. You can't precisely identify what is wrong. You can't put it into words, but you've sniffed something that doesn't smell good to you. If you discern something that doesn't seem helpful or appropriate for your child, don't hesitate to keep it out of his life. Tell him, "That's just not the sort of thing that we want to be part of our home."

Second, let's get serious about limiting the time our children spend in front of the television. It is possible to grow up without a television and not become a social leper. If you choose to have a television in your home, carefully restrict its use. Don't allow children to turn on the television without your permission. Make it clear that they do not have the right to watch whatever they please. I would urge parents not to allow children to watch television on a daily basis, even if there is unobjectionable programming each day. Daily television can easily become a daily habit, and children inevitably feel that they have a "right" to watch television. We try to limit television viewing to less than four hours per week in our family. When television is being viewed, watch it together, and help the children develop a perspective about what they are seeing. (For an excellent study on the effects of television, I recommend *Taming the TV Habit* by Kevin Perrotta [Servant Books: Ann Arbor, Michigan, 1982].) And remember to pay attention to the cartoons. Many of us grew up on cartoons and consider them one of the "safe" programming options for our children. Many of the cartoons have changed since you were parked in front of the TV on Saturday morning in the 1950s and 1960s. If you let your kids watch cartoons, know what they are watching. Don't send your children to a neighbor's house "for cartoons" unless you have every reason to trust that neighbor has good discernment and is in a position to exercise it.

Third, don't let your kids get into significant identification with various kiddie culture figures. The ones to be especially careful about are those that come with a wide range of paraphernalia capable of developing a little world of their own. We've considered some of the more recent cartoon-based figures already. But some of the old standbys are just as objectionable. Barbie dolls are a classic case.

Your little girl gets a Barbie doll, along with a few outfits, for Christmas. You have some relatives who were into Barbie dolls when they were girls, and they establish this as their common ground of communication with your daughter. Every time there is a gift-giving event, Barbie and Ken paraphernalia pop up. A doting uncle buys the "Barbie and Ken Dreamhouse" and the "Barbie and Ken Porsche." Grandma sends a Barbie and Ken video cassette. Before you know it, your little girl is into Barbie dolls. She doesn't just have this skinny, well-proportioned plastic doll lying around the toy box, pulled out from time to time. Barbie is part of her life. There is a Barbie and Ken sector in her room. Her fantasy is being shaped by Barbie and Ken.

Newsweek magazine reports that Bill Barton, the co-designer of the Barbie doll, which emerged in the late 1950s, has had second thoughts about what he brought into being.

> "Barbie has become an obsession with some little girls," says Barton, a silver haired grandfather.... He believes that the bosomy, wasp-waisted doll can promote unrealistic "beauty expectations" in youngsters. "If a child is less than attrac-

tive," he maintains, "she can develop a psychosis about this." Barton, 56, even attributes the current plague of anorexia (self-imposed starvation) in young women partly to Barbie's idealized slenderness. . . .

But, as the article reports, Barton sees some redeeming virtues in his creation. "The thousands of hours spent changing Barbie's many costumes," Barton suggests guilelessly, "may motivate some little girls to pursue an adult career in the fashion industry." However, when he adds up the advantages and disadvantages, common sense prevails. "Barton confesses that he has never given one of the dolls to his young granddaughters. 'It seems to me they've put more sex into it now,' he comments disapprovingly. 'I like little girls to stay little girls as long as they can.' "

It is not difficult to avoid objectionable kiddie culture toys entirely. It might take a word of caution to Grandma and Aunt Bernice around Christmas time, but it can be done. There are plenty of other toys that don't come with these trappings.

Fourth, we need to teach our children to be discerning. They need to understand that some things are fine and encouraged, some things are forbidden. Some things mom and dad don't like and won't let them get into. As the children are able, explain the reasons for exercising discernment and teach them the skills for doing it themselves.

Fifth, we cannot avoid the need to oversee the influence of their peers. Help your children to develop friendships with other children whose families support the values of your family, who share your concerns. That may mean investing the time and energy to invite children from across town to play or to drive your children to a friend's house rather than have them hang around with the neighborhood kids. But the value of developing committed relationships with other families who share your values provides many benefits.

If your child is spending time with a neighborhood chum

who is encouraging the wrong things, limit or, if necessary, eliminate the time they spend together. This can be difficult for all involved, but the alternative is more difficult. Get to know the children and families that your children play with. Before encouraging or allowing significant contact, have the child over to your house in order to get to know him or her better. It simply isn't possible to take a "hands off" approach to peers without compromising the call to raise our children in the discipline and instruction of the Lord.

"But don't our children have a responsibility to be light to the world and salt to the earth? Shouldn't they be reaching out to the neighborhood kids, even the ones who might exercise a negative influence on them?" you may be thinking.

While our children can have a positive influence on other children for the sake of the kingdom, we shouldn't be naive about who is influencing whom and what it actually takes for our children to be the influencers rather than the influenced. As adults, we know that it takes a fairly active approach to sharing our faith to overcome the tendency to be shaped by the values of those around us. Those who resist the drift are usually those who are active in reaching out.

Young children are often simply not capable of this kind of active approach to their peers. If we think that God wants to reach out to another child who might be the source of negative influence on our own children, we should be willing to invest the supervision that it takes to see that the influence is going in a positive direction. For example, one of our daughter's teachers made a point of assigning one of the more troubled children in her class to sit next to her because she was able to be loving and kind where other children were being mean. We were happy to allow that, because our daughter was able to do it without being drawn into the negative behavior. It was also a situation where an adult was present to provide effective supervision.

If we think that our children should be spending time with other kids who might well draw them in the wrong direction in order to be the light of the world, we should observe our kids in action. When our children are with peers who are not likely to exercise a good influence on them, what is really going on? Are our children overcoming the negative influence and really making a difference with their peers? It is one thing to avoid the uncomfortable decisions that can come with overseeing our children's peer influence with the vague hope that our kids are able to make a positive influence. But it is another thing to have the hope realized. We simply cannot afford to be naive about this issue.

Finally, we need to teach our children that being a disciple of Jesus means that we do some things differently than many other people. The fact is, we are raising our children during an age when Western culture based on Judeo-Christian values is in the process of collapsing. This means that children raised in Christian families (if the families are not simply yielding to the process of secularization) will be different from other children. They will do some things their peers are not doing and will not do some things considered normal by other children. So from an early age, it is necessary to prepare children for this. We let them know that, as Christians, we have a distinct way of life from many of the people around us. We aren't different for the sake of being different. We are different for the sake of obedience to Christ. We are not concerned about what other people think when we're different so much as we are concerned about what Christ thinks. Sometimes, the fact that we are different will cause us to feel uncomfortable, but that is part of the cost of following Jesus.

Young children do not normally object to this. They accept it as a fact of life. If it is settled in their hearts and minds early on, they will be better equipped to face some of the stronger challenges that await them as they grow older.

Light for Our Generation

The visitor from an African tribal village who preferred his environment for raising Christian children was right in discerning the cultural pressures that work on children in our society to separate them from God. But God has placed us in this environment to shine as lights. The power at work within us is indeed greater than the power at work in the world. If we are willing to walk in obedience to the teaching of Jesus, we will shine as lights in our generation. That's one of the most exciting aspects of the call to raise our children for Christ. Perhaps in no other time in the history of Western society has the quality of our family life—the distinctiveness of our child rearing and its results—been so key in being the light of Christ to those around us, a critical element of our savor as salt in the world.

Putting It into Practice: The Influence of Kiddie Culture

1. Determine how much time your children spend watching television each week. Without trying to change their viewing habits, keep a daily log for a week of TV time. Note the programs they watched during this period on the log. (You may need to keep a separate log for each child.)

2. How does the reality compare with what you think is appropriate for your children?
Note your answers to the following questions.

• How much TV, if any, per week should be allowed?

_____

• Which programs, if any, should be allowed?

_____

• What other rules for TV use should be established?

_____

_____

_____

3. Develop a plan for implementing what you wrote down in number two above. Consider the following questions:

• What changes do we, as parents, need to make in our television viewing in order to be models for our children?

• Should we change the location of the TV in our home to allow for more effective supervision? (Remember, removing it entirely is an option.)

• How do we want to implement a new approach—all at once or step by step?

Write your implementation steps in the space provided.

_____

_____

_____

_____

_____

_____

_____

_____

_____

_____

For Group Discussion and Support

1. What elements of kiddie culture have you observed?

2. Of those elements listed, were there any that surprised you?

3. Share with the group the one area you think needs most attention first in your situation.

4. End with prayer. Ask God for the discernment and help you need to free your children from the influence of kiddie culture. Close by interceding for all of the children in the families that make up your group. Encourage parents to pray out specific prayers for their children.

TEN

Sounding
the Same Note

JESUS SAID, "A house divided against itself cannot stand."
How truly he spoke! A house divided against itself cannot
stand, and a family divided against itself cannot stand. This is
one of the reasons the New Testament places such an emphasis
on the importance of unity in marriage, in the family, and in the
body of Christ. As we consider the challenge of raising
children in the modern world, this is a key issue—the need to
be united as husband and wife in our approach to child rearing.

Nancy and I aim to abide by a simple motto: speak with one
voice to the children. We try to be very careful not to contradict
each other when we give direction and leadership to the kids.
It's not always easy.

I remember the time I got into a difficult discussion with one
of the kids at dinner. I didn't realize it at the time, but the topic
under discussion was the cause of considerable embarrassment
to this child. Rather than contradict me openly, Nancy
graciously changed the subject and after dinner pointed out my
blunder. I was then able to work the matter out with the child
privately.

But sounding the same note is more than a matter of speech.
We try to avoid non-verbal contradictions as well. That

includes sighs, rolling one's eyes, and glaring at each other.

Speaking with one voice and avoiding contradiction between husband and wife is especially important when a child has a personal investment in the issue you're dealing with. Perhaps you disagree with the punishment being doled out by your spouse and communicate dissent in the child's presence. More often than not it only makes things worse. The child is more confused by the dispute between mom and dad than over the punishment itself. He is reinforced in the notion that the punishment is unfair and that his parents really don't know what they are doing. And we all know how competent children are at the age-old art of playing one parent against the other!

The "no contradiction in front of kids" rule is not absolute. Other concerns sometimes override it. Dad says it's O.K. to cross the street. But mom has a better vantage point and sees a car racing around the corner. Or dad, as head of the family, may need to overrule a direction given by his wife. But he should have a good reason for doing it. Fathers need to be very careful not to undermine mom's authority.

Now we all know that it takes more than this to speak consistently with one voice as you lead your children. It takes more than just effort not to contradict each other. Jesus said, "Out of the fullness of the heart, the mouth speaks." To speak consistently with one voice to your children requires a unity of mind and heart about raising children. The "outworked fullness" of that unity doesn't magically appear when you slip a ring on your spouse's finger at the altar and say "I do." It is a unity which is given to you as a gift, and it is something that must be worked out over time. Here are four keys Nancy and I have discovered in working out our unity as husband and wife in raising our family.

Key #1: A Common Vision

We need to look into the mirror of God's Word for a vision of who we are and what we are about. What are we to be?

Parents are meant to be an ordered partnership with a joint responsibility for a noble venture.

Consider for a moment God's purpose in creating a man and a woman to be husband and wife. Think of man and woman, Adam and Eve, before the stain and perversion of sin polluted God's purpose. God creates man and woman not just to skip naked through the garden, enjoying the creation and talking to the animals. He creates man and woman in his image because he wants them to represent him on the earth. God wants them to rule the virgin planet that he created. He wants them to preside over the creation. He wants them to be king and queen. He calls them to lead and care for things—to be shepherds, caretakers, providers, and presiders. He calls them to be fruitful and to multiply. Together they have responsibility to extend the kingdom of God. There is order in the partnership. Adam exercises leadership and Eve is designed as a helpmate. There is a complementarity within the partnership that has to do with the unique purpose in creating man male, and woman female. But they are partners, "joint heirs," as the apostle Peter says. They've been given a common gift. Together they inherit the same life and have a common mission that involves leadership and care for all that God gives them.

Yes, husbands and wives are partners in a noble venture! When we look into the mirror of God's Word—and we ought to look in that mirror long and hard and often—we see that we are a team with a joint responsibility in a noble venture. That's the first key because if we *see* ourselves as a team with a joint responsibility in a noble venture, we will begin to *act* like a team with a joint responsibility in a noble venture.

Key #2: Communication with Your Partner about the Noble Venture

If husband and wife are in fact a pastoral team, then the team has to have meetings. The team has to coordinate individual efforts for the common venture. The team has to review the films of past games and come up with a game plan for the future. That means husbands and wives need to set some time aside regularly to talk about the noble venture of raising their children.

What kind of time?

Daily time. The partnership should be in touch on a daily basis, able to discuss any pertinent issues involving the children. Judy needs some special attention from Mom today. Someone needs to drive the girls to their dentist appointment. These aren't necessarily serious discussions—just keeping in touch. For most of us, some kind of predictable pattern for this kind of communication is required. It may mean ten minutes after work or before bed, a call from the office at noon, or a brief chat after dinner. Do whatever works best for you and your schedule. But don't let it slide!

Weekly time. While the daily communication can cover the day-to-day matters of child rearing, it doesn't allow the kind of discussion that is required to handle a variety of concerns adequately. The kids seem to be getting sick a lot. What's going on? Jim has been getting under my skin lately, and I can't put my finger on it. Should we send Caroline to kindergarten this fall, or should we wait until next year?

For several years Nancy and I have gone out to breakfast once a week to plan and to talk about how things are going. With four children ages seven through seventeen, there always seems to be plenty to discuss. If we've been focusing on helping a particular child with a problem, we review how it's going. If we have different perspectives on how to handle something (What time should a fifteen-year-old go to bed?), we try to work it out. If we are stumped by one thing or another (How can we handle this constant bickering that has been going on lately among the kids?), we try to figure out where to get some help. If we've read a book or heard some teaching that applies to our family life, we talk it over.

Some folks take an hour and a half on Saturday or some time on Sunday evening. Some find that a lunch time every other week is sufficient. But some time, away from distractions, more or less weekly is a great help toward working out the kind of unity that allows husband and wife to sound a clear note for the sake of their children.

Effective communication on a weekly basis includes these elements: (1) Asking questions, sharing observations, and taking stock of how individual children are doing. How is Amy doing with obedience when Dad is gone? It's time to talk with Tommy about his temper, isn't it? Jenny feels like she doesn't have any friends. Why is this infant waking up seventeen times a night? (2) Identify the areas that need action now. There are plenty of things to handle, but we can't do everything at once. What are the things that we should be sure to address right now? (3) Develop a plan. This is a key to effective communication about the children—the difference between mere handwringing and leading. Whenever you talk about a problem area and decide that it really needs attention, try to answer the question, "What should we do about it?" Perhaps your plan is simply to keep a close eye on something and to review it in a couple of weeks or to seek out counsel from someone you trust. Whatever it is, be as specific as possible and follow through. (4) Evaluate and review progress concerning things you've discussed or planned for at previous meetings. (5) Keep a notebook to record agenda items and decisions. (6) Pray together for wisdom, for help, and for specific needs.

Yearly time. I was sitting around with a few other married men, and we were talking about how well some men do who are committed to living single for God when it comes to living out their ideal of life: what emphasis they place on taking time away from the normal rush of life to pray, the way they seek the Lord, the way they consider together how their common life is going and what the Lord is saying to them. "Hey!" we concluded, "Why shouldn't we take a weekend away with our wives each year to do the same for our families?" Well, there are always good reasons not to. Lining up babysitting for a weekend is no joke. Finding a free weekend isn't easy either.

But then we thought of those single men. They lead busy lives, too. Why does it work for them? Because they know they have to do it in order to keep their spiritual fervor, to be a committed body of brothers. They make it a priority and do it. So we decided to do it. We decided to take our wives away for a weekend each year to seek the Lord together, to intercede for the life of the family, to consider important long-range questions together.

If a weekend away is unworkable, try for a full Saturday away. If that won't work, a few evenings in a row with no other responsibilities might work.

Is our unity as husband and wife worth the time and effort that this pattern of communication requires? The apostle Paul said: "Make every effort to keep the unity of the Spirit through the bond of peace" (Eph 4:1).

Key #3: Draw from a Common Body of Wisdom

Most husbands and wives come together with different approaches to child rearing. There may be substantial similarities, but there are also substantial differences. My wife Nancy and I were born within twenty-four hours of each other. We were in neighboring nurseries and grew up within a few miles of each other. We each had a mom and a dad and two sisters. But the "culture" of our families was very different: the way of relating, the way of disagreeing, and the kinds of things we did together.

For instance, my mother is a master at indirect communication. At the dinner table, she wouldn't say, "Please pass me the bread," but, "I wonder if someone might pass the bread this way"; or even, "Marilyn, would you like some more bread? Glen, how about you? Well, then, I might have a piece." My mother-in-law, on the other hand, doesn't flinch from direct communication.

Just after we were married, for example, I was facing the age-old dilemma of what to call my in-laws: Mom and Dad, Mr.

and Mrs. Rozelle, or Stan and Dolores. At first, I didn't call them anything, which was a little awkward as you can imagine. Finally, my mother-in-law said to me, "Well Ken, what's it going to be? Dolores or Mom? Doesn't make much difference to me, but you'd better pick something." You must understand that to me this was unheard of. I am quite sure my mother would have died before dealing with a matter like that so straightforwardly. After recovering from the shock, I replied, "O.K., Mom."

Nancy and I have had to talk over the different communication styles that we've picked up from our families. In the case of direct versus indirect communication, I've learned to appreciate how helpful the more straightforward style of Nancy's mother can be. Nancy's adjusted to the fact that what seems "straightforward" to her can sometimes seem pushy to me.

A great deal of the disunity between husband and wife, especially in the area of child-rearing practices and approaches, can be traced to the fact that husband and wife are drawing wisdom from different wells. For those who share a common life in a church or community, the teaching of that body can provide a common source of wisdom. As much as possible, Nancy and I seek to draw wisdom from the same well. Together we consider the teaching of God's Word. Together we commit ourselves to his teaching. And we agree together on what that means in our family. We talk about the informal sources of wisdom that come from the way my folks used to do things, the way Nancy's folks used to do things. We talk about these things and decide how we think we should handle family matters.

We consider and agree together on whose personal advice we want to lean on. We can hear input from many individuals on child-rearing issues, and God can speak through any vessel he chooses. But there is a difference between hearing what someone has to say and leaning on what someone has to say. We should be especially discerning when it comes to the wisdom we lean on. Is it biblical? Is it true wisdom from God's Word? Does it make good sense? Does it work? Has it borne good fruit? Can we see confirming results in the lives of others? If the wife is getting personal advice concerning the children from her best friend, Jane, but the husband doesn't respect Jane's perspective on child rearing, the unity between them won't be built up. Husband and wife together need to draw from the same well.

Key #4: To be United with Your Partner Involves Walking in Ephesians 5.

In the Scriptures, headship and subordination are understood in the context of unity:

> Wives, submit to your husbands as to the Lord. For the husband is the head of the wife as Christ is the head of the church, his body, of which he is the Savior. (Eph 5:22-23)

They are a means to expressing and achieving unity. We see this in the unity of God himself. God is One: Father, Son, and Holy Spirit. And this unity is expressed in the subordination of the Son to the Father. We see this reflected in the unity between Christ and the church. Christ and the church are meant to be, above all things, united. Their unity is expressed through the headship of Christ and the subordination of the church. Wherever you see God laying out a pattern of headship and subordination, you can bet that he is interested in establishing unity. One of the chief reasons for headship and subordination in marriage is to insure that the unity of husband and wife is practically attainable. It's not just some mystical reality which is invisible because it cannot be lived out in flesh and blood. It is meant to be a working, functional unity of heart and mind, soul and body.

Practically speaking, husband and wife can agree on 95

percent of all decisions and approaches in regard to raising the children. But, if they are stalemated on the remaining 5 percent, if they are locked in an unresolvable power struggle over even a small number of concerns, considerable confusion can result.

It may be something as simple as bedtime for the kids. The child asks his parents, "What time do I have to go to bed tonight?" Mom says 9:00 and dad simultaneously answers 9:30. Upon quick reflection, mom or dad may decide that the other party has a better idea. But both may have good reasons for the answer they give. It is not as if they can suspend judgment until next week or let the child decide himself. So how is it settled? Dad is the leader of the pastoral team, so he makes the call and mom backs him up. On occasion it is wise to suspend a decision until you can reach a common mind through discussion. But who decides when an issue should be handled like that? Dad is the leader of the pastoral team, so he makes the call and mom backs him up. Otherwise, the unity of the team becomes quickly undermined. To have true unity, there has to be effective headship and subordination.

What recourse does a wife have when she feels the husband's decision is injurious? First of all, she can ask him to *reconsider*. Second, she can ask her husband to seek an *outside opinion*. She can ask him to consult with his pastor or a trusted advisor. A husband is wise to do this when his wife makes such a request. If the matter is serious, the wife *may consult the husband's pastoral leader*, even if her husband is not keen on the idea. Finally, she can take up the matter with *God, asking him to give wisdom* to her husband.

Conclusion

In a sense, this last chapter includes the first step in implementing the kind of training process I've described throughout this book—the weekly husband-and-wife meeting.

The great danger in writing a book of this sort is that the reader will be overwhelmed by the task at hand, paralyzed by too many good ideas. But if we can establish a weekly time to discuss child rearing with our spouse (or if single parents set aside a weekly time for prayer, reflection, and planning), we will have taken the most important practical step toward a more focused and purposeful approach to raising our children. Then, week by week, we can review, plan, and seek God's wisdom and help.

As we conclude, let's remember the words of the prophet Zechariah to a people faced with what seemed like an overwhelming task: "Who has despised the day of small things?" (Zec 4:10). Or consider Jesus' parable of the kingdom: "The kingdom of heaven is like leaven, which a woman took, and hid in three pecks of meal, until it was all leavened" (Mt 13:33 NASB). Or, again, recall Jesus' story about how the farmer's grain grows, "First the blade, then the head, then the mature grain in the head" (Mk 4:28 NASB).

The kingdom of God does not come instantaneously but progressively. It has small beginnings, but a glorious end. The work of raising children who are obedient to the call of the kingdom is a work of the kingdom. Like the kingdom, it unfolds progressively.

Let's also remember that God himself is with us to work in us and through us as parents. Many of us are deeply concerned about "doing a bad job" of child rearing. We are insecure about our competence and subject to discouragement. In fact, God has given us a challenging task and placed us in challenging times. Many supports that used to be available for raising children are gone. But God understands that and is prepared to make up the difference with his abiding presence and his saving help. He is not a God far off, folding his arms and shaking his head in disgust as we stumble along trying to raise these kids. He is Immanuel. He is "God-With-Us," "God-For-Us." Let's not pretend that we can get by on our own. The simple truth is we can't. Instead, let's approach the task of raising our children by acknowledging both our need and his presence.

Putting It into Practice: Sounding the Same Note

1. Decide to set aside a regular (weekly or twice monthly) time to meet as a team to discuss the noble venture. Review the guidelines presented in the chapter under "Weekly Time."

You don't have a plan until you have specific answers to the following questions:

What day of the week? _____

What time? _____

Where? _____

Babysitting plan (if needed) _____

First scheduled meeting date (this is the real thing!):

_____

2. List one thing you do that has the effect of undermining unity with your spouse:

_____

List one thing your spouse does that you think has the effect of undermining unity (be kind!):

_____

3. Share your answers to the questions above with your spouse and discuss. Begin by sharing your own perceived fault.

• Remember, be as understanding of your spouse's perceived fault as you would like him or her to be of yours.

• Be as willing to have your fault dealt with as you would like your spouse to be willing to have his or her fault dealt with.

For Group Discussion and Support

1. Share ideas about how to get free for a regular husband-wife meeting, or if you are a single parent, a regular planning time.

2. Do members of the group wish to exchange babysitting assignments to support the goal of a regular husband-wife meeting for all the couples in the group?

3. What do you find to be the most challenging aspect of sounding the same note in childrearing issues?

4. Pray for the power to "maintain the unity of the Spirit in the bond of peace" (Eph 4:1). Pray for practical help in solving obstacles faced by any members of the group in establishing a regular time for discussion and planning of family issues.

Other Books on Marriage and Family Life From Servant Publications

Husbands, Wives, Parents, Children
Ralph Martin

A Christian family needs a lot more than communication techniques or discipline tips to flourish in today's society. Ralph Martin offers more. He describes a whole way of life rooted in Christian principles, then shows how to live that life in a non-Christian world. This book can help any couple strengthen their marriage and family. Martin examines all aspects of a husband and wife's relationship with each other and with their children—from sexual love to authority in the home. $7.95

10 Weeks to a Better Marriage
Randall and Therese Cirner

Marriages can always get better. You and your spouse can grow closer; your commitment to each other can be stronger; and your life together can be richer. In *Ten Weeks to a Better Marriage*, Randall and Therese Cirner show you how to improve the most intimate of all human relationships. Their 10-week program is scriptural, active, practical, well-organized, systematic, and just plain fun. The best news about *Ten Weeks to a Better Marriage* is that it is based on the good news. The program works because it shows you how to seek God's plan for marriage as revealed in Scripture and how to open yourself to the power of the Holy Spirit. Why wait? $8.95